The Good Food of Szechwan

MANCHURIA

Amur R.

Liao R.

INNER MONGOLIA

NINGSIA

Peking ○
Tientsin ○

HOPEI

KANSU

SHANSI

Yenan ○

SHANTUNG

TSINGHAI

Huang Ho R.

KIANGSU

SHENSI

HONAN

Yangchow ○

Nanking ○
Wuhsi ○
Soochow ○
Shangha

Tuojiang R.

Fujiang R.

Jialingjiang R.

SZECHWAN

HUPEH

ANHWEI

SIKANG

Chengtu ○

Yangtze R.

Hangchow ○
Ning ○

CHEKIANG

Chungking ○

Changsha ○

KIANGSI

HUNAN

Foochow ○

KWEICHOW

FUKIEN

T

YUNNAN

Si Kiang R.

KWANGSI

KWANGTUNG

Swatow ○

TAIWAN

Kaohs ○

Canton ○

Irawaddy R.

Macao ○
Hong Kong ○

Mekong R.

SOUTH CHINA SEA

PHILIPPIN

The Good Food of Szechwan

Down-to-Earth Chinese Cooking

Robert A. Delfs

Photography by Keizō Kaneko

Kodansha International Ltd.

Tokyo, New York and San Francisco

Distributed in the United States by Kodansha International/USA Ltd. through Harper & Row, Publishers, Inc., 10 East 53rd Street, New York, New York 10022.

Published by Kodansha International Ltd., 12-21, Otowa 2-chome, Bunkyo-ku, Tokyo 112 and Kodansha International/USA Ltd., 10 East 53rd Street, New York, New York 10022 and 44 Montgomery Street, San Francisco, California 94104. Copyright © in Japan 1974 by Kodansha International Ltd. All rights reserved. Printed in Japan.

LCC 74-77960
ISBN 0-87011-231-7
ISBN 4-7700-0444-3 (in Japan)

First edition, 1974
Eighth printing, 1981

CONTENTS

GUIDE TO ROMANIZATION:

The Pinyin system of romanization is used for all the names of recipes, ingredients and cooking techniques in this book. It appears that the Pinyin system will enjoy wider currency as time goes on because it has been officially adopted by the People's Republic of China. However, names of places and historical personages, where they do occur, are rendered according to a modified Wade-Giles system or romanization which has been customarily used in the West.

The following guide will enable one who is unfamiliar with Chinese pronunciation to voice a reasonable facsimile.

VOWELS:

a as in f*a*ther

ai, diphthong like the *i* in h*i*gh

ao, diphthong like the *ow* in h*ow*

ang like the *ong* in s*ong*

ei, diphthong as in n*ei*ghbor

e as in m*e*n

i as in mach*i*ne

o as in n*o*rth

ong, the *o* is pronounced like the *oo* in l*oo*m

ou, diphthong like the *oe* in d*oe*

u as in tr*u*e

CONSONANTS are generally pronounced as in English. The following are additional guides:

c like the *ts* in le*t's*

ch as in *ch*eck

g as in *g*ate

j as in *j*ump

q like the *ch* in *ch*ill

s as in *s*ing

sh as in *sh*e

x as in a combination of *h* and *sh*; an aspirated *hs* sound

y as in *y*oung

z like the *ds* in lan*ds*

zh like the *j* in *J*ill

FOREWORD

I think I should begin this book by explaining why and how it came to be written, particularly as it may seem strange or inappropriate that an American pose as the "author" of a Chinese cookbook. Frankly, I do not consider myself the creator of any of the recipes in this book. I have seen my role as that of a transmitter of information about cooking techniques that have been largely unavailable in the English language up to now.

I have begun by giving general information about Chinese cooking, its ingredients and methods. The recipes are a collection of those that seem the most broadly representative of the food of Szechwan Province and that are feasible to reproduce in a Western kitchen. This list was broadened to include as well a few recipes drawn from the culinary traditions of northern and eastern China which are not widely known in the West as yet.

For the recipes, I compared as many Chinese-language versions of the same dish as possible, deriving a final recipe which, in my opinion, was both reasonably practical and authentic (bearing in mind that there are numerous "authentic" ways to make any kind of food). The directions for preparation have been supplied in a much more detailed and expanded form than would ordinarily be the case in a Chinese-language cookbook, in consideration of the techniques and skills which are common knowledge to cooks in China but which cannot be assumed for Western readers. My objective has been to try to introduce these recipes in an authentic form with instructions which are comprehensive and clear. The book is intended for people who like to eat and cook good food and who like to know something about what they are eating.

My experience with Szechwanese cooking dates from 1970, when I spent a year in Taipei, Taiwan, studying Chinese. During that year I ate almost exclusively at the many Szechwanese restaurants in that city. I also briefly attended a cooking class and obtained personal instruction from a number of generous and skilled cooks whose restaurants I frequented.

This book itself originally grew out of a Christmas present—a short mimeographed pamphlet of Szechwanese recipes which I sent to friends in December, 1973. The response, which was suprisingly good, led to my expanding my work into its present form.

Robert A. Delfs

June, 1974
Tokyo

INTRODUCTION

CHINA'S REGIONAL CUISINES

The unique way in which the Chinese peoples have interacted with each other through history has often been described in terms of "diversity within unity," a formula that might be extended to the various regional styles of Chinese cooking. In its vastness, China encompasses a wide range of geographic and climatic conditions. The culture of the Chinese people as well has exhibited a richness and variety that we in the West are only beginning to recognize. It is only natural, then, that these differences are expressed in local traditions of cooking—each as distinctive and as popular as the numerous types of European cuisines.

The cooking of China is usually divided into four major regional groupings—northern, southern, eastern and western. Each of these can be further divided into typical local styles of cooking. Northern, or Mandarin cooking, is the food of the great wheat-growing northern plain. In particular, the cuisine of the capital Peking was greatly influenced by Mongolian preferences during the Manchu, or Ch'ing, dynasty (1644–1912). Northern cooking is famed for its use of lamb and beef and dishes that are often served with heavy and spicy sauces.

The Chinese cooking most familiar to Americans is Cantonese, which is one of the cooking styles of the southern coastal region. Its popularity in the West is due in part to the fact that the majority of Chinese immigrants to the West have come from the region of Canton in Kwangtung Province. Southern cooking relies heavily on seafood and tropical produce and emphasizes the natural flavors of foods by using lightly seasoned, rich sauces.

Eastern cooking refers to the foods of the northern Pacific coast and the lower regions of the Yangtze River. Shanghai cooking is the best known of all the eastern styles but the cuisines of the cities of Ningpo, Soochow and Nanking, among others, are considered equally developed and distinctive. Less spicy than northern or western cooking, eastern foods are prepared with large amounts of oil. Fresh and saltwater fish figure greatly in this cuisine, noted for its many entrees served at room temperature.

Finally, there is the west and the province of Szechwan, a great mountain-ringed basin. Thanks to its very rich soil and temperate climate, Szechwan historically has been one of the most prosperous regions of China, and its major crops of rice and oil-bearing grains can be farmed almost year round. Incorporated into the Chinese Empire by 300 B.C., Szechwan was extensively settled by Han Chinese from the north and is today China's most densely populated province. Ethnically, linguistically and culturally, the people of Szechwan can be regarded as directly related to northerners, but the geography of their province has accounted for a high degree of isolation. The mountains that surround the province have been a significant barrier to transportation, which was limited to narrow mountain roads and the treacherous upper reaches of the Yangtze River.

Hearty and flavorful Szechwanese food is the best known of the western styles of cooking. Most of the basic foodstuffs used in Szechwan cooking are familiar to the American or European table, unlike the exotic ingredients commonly used in the cooking of tropical, marine areas such as the region of Canton. The most striking feature of Szechwanese food is the liberal use of red peppers, fresh ginger, garlic and the spice known as Szechwan pepper. However, not all Szechwanese food is hot or spicy.

In addition to the broad categories sketched above, one should also mention the special vegetarian cuisines developed by Buddhists. There are also special foods of the various national minorities of China, especially Mongolian and Moslem cooking.

THE FLAVORS OF SZECHWANESE COOKING

We can get a more accurate picture of what Szechwanese food actually is by thinking somewhat systematically about Chinese cooking. The advantage of doing so is that we can gain a sense of the possibilities and limits involved, the factors which are manipulated and how this is done. Cooking can be thought of as a kind of technology and within China there exists a body of information, some of it centuries old, which might be called a "theory" or "theories" of cooking. While these so-called theories should not be over-emphasized, it remains true that a large number of Chinese cooks have been in some way aware of them.

The basic method of cooking in China is to fry foods in oil, either vegetable or animal. By using oil it is possible to bring the food to a very high temperature, very quickly, both cooking the food and sterilizing it. Cooking with oil also releases oil-soluble flavoring substances that are absorbed into the oil and are quickly distributed throughout the dish. Red peppers especially, but also fresh ginger, garlic and green onion contain both water-soluble and oil-soluble flavorings of perceptibly different tastes. Water is used to boil, poach or steam food and also serves to release, distribute and hold water-soluble flavorings in sauces and soups. Starch products of various kinds are used to thicken water and oil-based sauces so that they adhere to the food, usually with a light glaze rather than as a thick gravy. With water-and-oil sauces, cornstarch or flour serves as an emulsifier, inhibiting the separation of the water and oil. Sugar is also occasionally used as a thickener.

The practice of employing extremely high heat in cooking with oil can probably be traced to the widespread use of coal as a cooking and heating fuel in China. The preferred stove of a professional Chinese cook bears a striking resemblance to a blast furnace, to my mind. Traditionally, baking is almost unknown, and the practice of broiling or roasting over hot coals or an open fire seems to be very rare, due to the fact that the commonly used fuel was coal, not wood. However, meats and poultry are often smoked, usually very quickly and only partially, the main purpose being to flavor the food rather than to preserve it for storage.

In Chinese, the general methods of cooking are as follows:

炒	chao	To fry in a relatively small amount of oil at a high temperature. Occasionally to heat without oil or water.
炸	zha	Usually to deep fry. Occasionally to fry at a very high temperature.
爆	bao	To fry very quickly at a very high temperature. Occasionally to cook thoroughly.
煮·烹	zhu (or peng)	To boil or poach.
燒	shao	To cook in a small amount of water. Also to braise.
蒸	reng	To steam.

In addition to these general methods, which have currency throughout China, there are traditionally considered to be seven flavors and eight methods of preparation that are particularly associated with Szechwanese cooking. The seven traditional flavors that are imparted to food either during the cooking process or by means of an accompanying sauce are listed below.

酸	suan	sour	The taste of vinegar.
辣	la	hot	The taste of red peppers. Occasionally the taste of black or Szechwan pepper.
麻	ma	sesame/peppery	The flavor of sesame, imparted by its seeds or oil. Also the pepperiness of black or Szechwan pepper.
苦	ku	bitter	The taste of green onion or leek.
甜	tian	sweet	Sweetness, from sugar or honey.
香	xiang	fragrant	The taste of garlic and/or ginger.
鹹	xian	salty	Saltiness, from salt or soy sauce.

A few more categories might supplement this list. The presence of sweet bean sauce, or tian-mian jiang (甜麵醬), might place a dish in the jiang (醬) category, as this word is used in the names of recipes calling for this ingredient. Another flavor group would indicate the use of aromatic star anise, or ba-jiao (八角). Furthermore, the category of la, or hot, could be subdivided to indicate the presence of hot bean sauce, or la-dou-ban jiang (辣豆瓣醬), in contrast to the use of fresh or dried red peppers. With these few additions, this scheme describes the combinations of flavors which characterize almost every recipe in this book.

Two other ingredients should be mentioned here. Chinese wine, produced from rice, is frequently used to soften or smooth out other flavors, but it is not used in sufficient quantity to merit a flavor category of its own. Similarly, the taste of soy sauce, while distinct from that of salt, is not present in Szechwanese cooking to such an extent as to create a strong "soy" taste.

The so-called eight methods of preparation associated with Szechwanese cooking are listed below. These names are, in effect, shorthand recipes, indicating not only the manner of cooking but also suggesting the kind and relative strength of the flavorings to be used. Moreover, they are incorporated in the names of the recipes themselves much as terms such as "au gratin," "sauté" and "à la vinaigrette" are used in the names of

French recipes. At least one recipe using each of these eight methods has been included in this book.

Gan-shao (乾燒) means to simmer or poach meat, fish or vegetables in soup stock with wine and spices (hot bean sauce, chopped garlic and soy sauce) until the liquid has cooked down. Then, sugar, vinegar, green onion and a thickening agent are added. Sometimes the food is fried briefly before simmering. *Gan-shao* dishes are usually not very hot. The slow cooking process produces a thick sauce and the various flavorings penetrate the main ingredient. Often used with bland fish or vegetables.

Yu-xiang (魚香) literally means "fish fragrance," but in fact the term has nothing to do with fish. It describes food which is first fried or deep fried, then cooked with liberal amounts of chopped garlic, ginger and hot bean sauce. Green onion, a little sugar, wine and occasionally vinegar and Szechwan pepper are added as final ingredients. The food is stained a deep reddish brown by the hot bean sauce. *Yu-xiang* dishes are very hot and spicy and sometimes slightly sweet and sour.

Suan-la (酸辣), "sour" and "hot." Made with lots of vinegar, Szechwan pepper or occasionally red peppers, plus wine and soy sauce.

Ma-la (麻辣) means "peppery" as in Szechwan pepper and "hot" as in red peppers. The presence of ginger, green onion, soy sauce and a small amount of sugar is implied. The *ma-la* preparation tends to stain the foods a light brown color.

Gan-chao (乾炒) or *gan-bian* (乾煸), "dry-fried." As in *gan-shao* cooking (above), most of the ingredients in *gan-chao* dishes are usually cooked together from the beginning, though the main ingredient may be precooked. The food is fried over a high flame with oil, and no additional liquid (soup stock) is added. Foods are cooked longer than in normal stir-frying, or *chao* (炒), but not as long as in *gan-shao* cooking. *Gan-chao*, or *gan-bian*, dishes may be flavored with red peppers, Szechwan pepper, hot bean sauce, garlic, green onion, sugar and wine—or a combination of these. Because of the relatively long cooking time, the food is well-done, often crispy and deeply colored.

Guai-wei (怪味), literally "strange taste." This method, like the following two, is the name for a sauce that is prepared and poured over any cooked food, but usually poultry. "Strange taste" refers to the sauce that is said to incorporate and balance the flavors of sweetness, sourness, hotness, saltiness, and spiciness, while emphasizing none. *Guai-wei* sauce (see the recipe on page 51) is made with sesame oil and sesame paste, as well as Szechwan pepper, garlic, green onion, vinegar, sugar, red oil and soy sauce. The mixture is not cooked.

Jiao-ma (椒麻), or "pepper and sesame," indicates that Szechwan pepper and sesame oil or sesame paste dominate the sauce. Soy sauce, green onion, ginger and sugar are also used. The Szechwan pepper makes the *jiao-ma* sauce aromatic, and also slightly tart. Uncooked, to be poured over food which has been cooked.

Hong-you (紅油) means "red oil." Red-pepper oil dominates this sauce in which sugar, green onion, garlic, ginger, sesame paste and soy sauce may also be used. Uncooked, to be poured over cooked food.

Remember that this is a traditional listing, and in no way exhausts all the methods of preparing Szechwanese foods, some of which have been developed relatively recently. The best picture can be gained by looking over the recipes in this book, bearing in mind that the procedures described above are generalized from the specific instances given.

This discussion has been only a short introduction to the wide variety of Chinese regional cuisines and to the flavors and methods of Chinese and Szechwanese cooking. Here are listed a few books that I have consulted with profit. (Romanization for Chinese names is given according to the Wade-Giles system.)

Ch'en Chien-min. *Chūgoku ryōri gijutsu nyūmon (An Introduction to the Techniques of Chinese Cooking)*. Tokyo: 1968. This Japanese-language book contains exhaustive and detailed instructions on the preparation of numerous dishes, most of which are quite unusual and elaborate. Excellent information on materials, techniques, etc.

Tuan Feng-go. *Shih-yung shih-p'u (The Practical Cookbook)*. Taipei: 1970. A large selection of Chinese dishes from many regions with well-organized and easy-to-follow instructions.

Ye Jung-hwa. *Chung-kuo ming-ts'ai da-ch'uan (The Complete Collection of Famous Chinese Dishes)*. Hong Kong: 1968. This systematic work contains extensive selections of Cantonese, Pekinese and Szechwanese cooking. Equally large selections of recipes from Foochow, Ningpo, Shanghai and Yangchow. These emphasize the most distinctive and sometimes most elaborate dishes from each area, though many recipes would be difficult to make in a Western kitchen. The Szechwanese section has been reprinted in paperback as *Chang-tsung ch'uan-ts'ai p'u (The Cookbook of Authentic Szechwanese Food)*. Hong Kong: 1972.

————. *Da-chung ts'ai-p'u (The Masses Cookbook)*. Peking: 1973. A revised edition of the 1966 *Da-chung t'ang ts'ai p'u*, this book contains a large number of recipes submitted by municipal or commune food service centers throughout China.

————. *Wei ch'uan shih-p'u (The Wei Ch'uan Cookbook)*. Taipei: n.p.d. Issued by the home economics division of the Wei Ch'uan Food Company, the book is divided into three sections of Cantonese, Szechwanese and Taiwanese cooking. The directions to the recipes are very brief and often vague as to exact measures.

INGREDIENTS

Most large Chinatowns in the U.S. have a store that stocks ingredients used in northern and western Chinese dishes. Stores that serve smaller Asian-American communities are apt to have only Cantonese-style ingredients, but they may be able to order things for you. In many cases, the proprietors of Chinese grocery stores will speak Cantonese or other southern dialects, which means that they will pronounce Chinese words differently than the Peking pronunciation given here according to the Pinyin romanization system. If you must ask for assistance, it may be best to have the Chinese characters of the item you want written down on a piece of paper.

Not all the following entries are exclusive to Szechwanese cooking, and a few of the more common items may be available at large supermarkets that have Oriental foods sections.

BAMBOO SHOOT (*sun*, 筍)
Canned bamboo shoot is satisfactory and the only available substitute for fresh bamboo shoot. Rinse thoroughly before using. Canned bamboo, once it is opened, will keep for about a week if refrigerated in water. Change the water daily.

BEAN CURD: See DOU-FU.

BEAN SPROUTS (*dou-ya*, 豆芽)
The sprouts of mung beans, these pale-green sprouts are available fresh at Chinese grocery stores or health food stores. Or you can grow your own at home quite easily if you are around to water them 4 times a day. Delicate in taste and crisp in texture, they are very good stir-fried with shredded meat or with other vegetables. Parboiled briefly, they also make a good salad. Fresh bean sprouts will keep 4 to 5 days if covered with water and refrigerated (change the water daily). To freeze, wash and parboil the bean sprouts for 1–2 minutes. Drain well, place in containers and freeze. Thaw completely before using. This vegetable is also available canned. Wash well and drain before using.

CHINESE CABBAGE (*bai-cai*, 白菜)
An extremely versatile whitish-green leaf vegetable that can be stir-fried with poultry, meat or seafood and used in soups as well. Available at some supermarkets and most Chinese grocery stores. Keeps several days. Store as you would lettuce.

DOU-FU (豆腐)
This protein-rich food is made from an extract of soy beans by a process that is analogous to the manufacture of cheese. *Dou-fu* is considered to be an inexpensive meat substitute

in Asia. In America, it is likely to be almost as expensive per gram of protein as meat, but still much cheaper in terms of bulk. *Dou-fu* is sold in cakes, either individually packaged or kept under water. It keeps for a few days in water (it is best to change the water daily), but may not be frozen. There is a canned Japanese brand of *dou-fu* and also various mixes. It is also possible to make homemade *dou-fu*.

FERMENTED BLACK BEANS (*duo-chi*, 豆豉)
Small, soft, preserved soy beans that have a very pungent odor. Use very sparingly to heighten the flavor of poultry or meat and to subdue fishiness in seafood. Soak 10 minutes in cold water, rinse thoroughly and drain before using. Often sold in unlabeled plastic bags. This ingredient doesn't last indefinitely, so don't buy too much. Store in a tightly sealed container.

FIVE SPICES (*wu-xiang*, 五香)
Also known as Five-flavored Powder or Five-fragrance Spice Powder. Sold ready-mixed at Chinese grocery stores. A combination of star anise, anise pepper, fennel, cloves and cinnamon. Substitute allspice or try mixing equal parts of powdered cinnamon, clove, ginger and nutmeg. Use sparingly as a seasoning for whole-cooked poultry or roasted meat.

FRESH GINGER (*jiang*, 薑)
Ginger is used in fairly large quantities in Szechwanese cooking. Although this potato-like root vegetable is occasionally available in supermarkets, in most cases you'll have to buy it at Chinese grocery stores. Choose firm pieces with large sections—the smaller buds are usually waste. The younger the root, the juicier the ginger. When you use it, cut off a section (depending on how much you need), peel, and cut or chop according to instructions. When a recipe calls for a slice of ginger, it means a piece of ginger about 1-inch in diameter and 1/8-inch thick. Store as you would potatoes—in a cool, dry place—or if you cover unwashed, unpeeled ginger with plastic wrap and refrigerate it, it will keep about 3 weeks. Ginger can also be frozen (don't wash or peel it). Cut off what you will need before it thaws and return the remaining ginger root to the freezer immediately. Powdered ginger is not a substitute but candied ginger with the syrup washed off or presoaked dried ginger for use in small quantities will pass.

NOODLES (*mian*, 麵)
Noodles are best bought fresh at the Chinese grocery store although certain types may be made at home. See pages 106 and 115 for a brief description of several kinds of noodles and their uses.

HOT BEAN SAUCE (*la-dou-ban jiang*, 辣豆瓣醬)
This is by far the most essential ingredient for Szechwanese cooking, providing a key flavoring as well as hotness, for a majority of Szechwanese dishes. There is no substitute. The canned varieties from Taiwan are not the best—poor enough, in fact, to justify almost any effort to obtain the real thing. The best I know of is made in the People's Republic of China and comes in jars with a colorful label showing giant red peppers in the foreground and a harbor scene in the background. The Wei Ch'uan Company in Taiwan makes a pretty fair hot bean sauce, which comes in a jar. The strength and saltiness of this ingredient vary considerably from brand to brand so the measures

of hot bean sauce and salt in the individual recipes may have to be adjusted to taste. For example, the Wei Ch'uan brand is extremely salty so, if you use that type, you may want to omit some of the salt called for in the recipe. Hot bean sauce need not be refrigerated but should be kept in a tightly sealed jar. If the surface becomes grayish, just stir it up from the bottom. Will keep for several months.

Hot pepper sauce (*la-jiao jiang*, 辣椒醬)
Not to be confused with hot bean sauce (*la-dou-ban jiang*) above, this is usually used as a table seasoning.

Mushrooms, dried (*dong-gu*, 冬菇)
Available in almost all Asian grocery stores. Soak in warm water to soften before using. Rinse and drain and cut away the tough stems. (Sometimes but infrequently you may be able to find fresh Chinese-type mushrooms instead of the dried variety.) Store in a cool, dry place.

Mushrooms, straw (*cao-gu*, 草菇)
These are available canned, if at all. Fresh button mushrooms taste different, but may be substituted.

Orange peel, dried (*chen-pi*, 陳皮)
Brown chips of dried orange peel give a unique, cinnamon-spicy flavor to poultry and meat. Sold in bulk or in unlabeled plastic bags. Unless otherwise specified, soak in warm water, and rinse and drain before using. Scrape residue off the inside of the peel.

Red oil (*la-you*, 辣油)
Also known as hot oil, this is a red-colored, red-pepper-flavored oil, usually sold in small bottles. Generally used as a table seasoning, it is occasionally used in cooking. Keeps indefinitely unrefrigerated.

Red peppers (*la-jiao*, 辣椒)
A frequently used ingredient in Szechwanese cooking, these small, red chili peppers sometimes are available fresh on the stalk at Chinese grocery stores. However, you will probably have to buy dried red peppers, called *gan la-jiao* (乾辣椒), which are sold in bulk or in small quantities in unlabeled plastic bags. Some recipes require dried red peppers to be soaked in warm water then seeded before using. In any case, whether you are using fresh or dried red peppers, handle them as little as possible and wash your hands thoroughly with soap after cutting or seeding them. The oils from the uncooked ingredient are quite strong and may prove irritating. Store dried red peppers in a sealed container or hang fresh or dried ones in a cool, dry place, as you would garlic.

Scallops, dried (*gan-bei*, 乾貝)
Salty and fibrous dried sea scallops are sold at Chinese grocery stores. About 1-inch in diameter, they are light brown in color and lend a rich flavor to soups and other dishes. Should be soaked in warm water before using. Very expensive. Substitute fresh or canned sea scallops.

Shrimp, dried (*kai-yang*, 開洋)
Small, shelled dried shrimp add flavor to soups and vegetable dishes. They are often sold in bulk or in unlabeled plastic bags. Soak in warm water to soften before using.

SESAME OIL (*zhi-ma you*, 芝麻油)

This is essential and usually easy to find since it is used in other styles of Chinese cooking as well as in Japanese cooking. Sesame oil usually serves as a seasoning, not as a cooking oil. You can often find it in health food stores.

SESAME PASTE (*zhi-ma jiang*, 芝麻醬)

Sesame paste is used only in a few dishes, but these are so good that this ingredient should be considered a necessity. Canned varieties from Taiwan and Hong Kong are usually available and there is also a People's Republic of China product, which comes in a jar. Sesame paste tends to separate and to settle in the bottom of the jar. If it is too hard to stir, you can rehomogenize it by heating the jar in water in a saucepan over low heat. You can substitute the sesame paste sold in American health food stores.

SNOW PEAS (*ho-lan dou*, 荷蘭豆)

Available fresh at Chinese grocery stores and sometimes frozen at supermarkets. Break off tips and remove strings before stir-frying.

SOY SAUCE (*jiang-you*, 醬油)

Chinese soy sauce is thinner than the Japanese-style soy sauce that is usually available in the U.S., but the difference is not critical. If the soy flavor seems too pronounced, reduce the amount of soy in any given recipe. You may also be able to buy the light grade of Japanese soy sauce (called *usukuchi shōyu* in Japanese), which is very close in taste to Chinese soy sauce.

STAR ANISE (*ba-jiao*, 八角)

This is a star-shaped, brown, woody-appearing seed cluster about 1-inch wide with an unmistakable licorice smell. Star anise is often sold in bulk or in unlabeled plastic bags. It is used in beef dishes. Do not substitute Western-type anise.

SWEET BEAN SAUCE (*tian-mian jiang*, 甜麵醬)

This fragrant bean puree is used in numerous pork dishes and is a staple in Peking-style cooking. Sweet bean sauce does not keep indefinitly, so don't buy too much and refrigerate it.

SZECHWAN PEPPER (*hua-jiao*, 花椒)

These are brown, sometimes reddish, peppercorns that have a pleasant, aromatic smell, reminiscent of pine. This spice is used frequently but sparingly in Szechwanese cooking to season meat and poultry and to make salt-and-pepper mixes. Most Chinese grocery stores stock this ingredient, which is sold in bulk or in unlabeled plastic bags. Grind the peppercorns in a pepper mill, coffee grinder or mortar before using. Toast slightly in a dry *wok* to facilitate grinding. Set aside some whole ones to use in recipes that call for peppercorns. Avoid using black pepper as a substitute.

SZECHWAN VEGETABLE (*zha-cai*, 榨菜)

This ingredient is also known as Szechwan radish or Szechwan chile radish. It is usually sold in cans with English labels but it may also be sold in bulk. Look for a twisted, dark olive vegetable, about the size of a small green pepper with reddish pickling paste adhering to it. Wash off the pickling material before using. Szechwan vegetable is extremely salty so never add salt when using it. Keep it in a tightly sealed container. Refrigerate.

Transparent vermicelli (*fen-tiao*, 粉條)

This is a type of thin-stranded noodle made from mung beans. Sold in packages by weight, the noodles are dried, rigid, silvery threads arranged in skeins from 8 to 14-inches long. Commonly used in soups and also as the base for one very famous Szechwanese dish, *Ma-yi Shang Shu* (see page 108). Place the noodles in boiling water briefly (until the threads become soft and translucent) and then drain before using. After they have softened, cut the noodles into manageable lengths before adding to soup, otherwise they are almost impossible to separate.

Vinegar (*cu*, 醋)

Chinese rice vinegar is available in bottles and comes in two varieties, white and red, both of which are weaker and less strongly flavored than Western types. Japanese rice vinegar is essentially the same as Chinese white vinegar. Avoid using cider or wine vinegar. If you have to substitute, use white cider vinegar and reduce the measure by half.

Water chestnuts (*bi-ji*, 荸薺)

This bulb-type vegetable is about the size of a large walnut. Its flesh is white and crispy, and this ingredient is often used to add a crunchy texture to stir-fried dishes. While fresh water chestnuts (brown and unpeeled) will be difficult to find, canned varieties are quite available. Wash and rinse canned water chestnuts thoroughly before using. Will keep about a week if covered with water in a tighly sealed jar and refrigerated (change the water every 2 days).

Wine (*jiu*, 酒)

Used mainly in marinades or for seasoning, Chinese rice wine is preferred. Japanese saké is acceptable. Medium-dry or pale-dry sherry is a substitute.

Winter melon (*dong-gua*, 冬瓜)

Large, round, thick-skinned melon. Frosty green on the outside. White and pulpy on the inside. Often sold in sections in Chinese grocery stores. To store, cover the cut surfaces with plastic wrap and refrigerate. Will last 3 to 5 days.

Wood ear (*mu-er*, 木耳)

Also called cloud ear. A fungus, related to the mushroom, grown on the bark of trees. Don't try to pick your own—Western tree fungus is entirely different. Wood ear is often sold in bulk or in unlabeled plastic bags at Chinese grocery stores. The pieces look like curly, dried, gray black leaves. Should be soaked in warm water and rinsed thoroughly before using. Cut away and discard any tough parts. It may be added optionally to any number of dishes and is very good in soups.

UTENSILS

WOK AND COVER: The round-bottomed *guo*, or as it has become popularly known in the West by its Cantonese pronunciation, the *wok*, is universal to all Chinese cooking. It serves as a frying pan, saucepan, deep fryer and pot all-in-one. With the addition of bamboo steaming trays or a rack and cover, it can be a steamer as well.

While it is possible to make any of the recipes in this book using a frying pan or whatever utensil corresponds to the function indicated, the *wok* is preferred, especially for stir-frying. Cooking oil collects at the bottom and is used more efficiently. The high, smooth sides make quick-stirring and cleaning easy and reduce the amount of food which ends up on the stove instead of on a plate.

I prefer the ugly black cast iron or steel *wok* to the shiny stainless steel or aluminum type for the same reason that I prefer a cast iron frying pan. The slightly porous iron absorbs a certain amount of oil, and under most circumstances, food never sticks. *Woks* come in two styles—one with "ear-type" handles on both sides, the other with a single, long, straight handle of iron or sometimes of wood. The single-handled version is easier to use. Picking up the double-handled *wok* or holding it with one hand can be difficult, and it is easy for a finger to miss the potholder. There is also some variety in the curvature of the *wok*. I prefer the shallower kind, but it's purely a matter of taste.

Choose a size of *wok* in accordance with your stove, storage area and the amount of food you will normally be preparing. A *wok* about 12-inches in diameter and 5-inches high or slightly larger is adequate for most home-cooking purposes.

A *wok* cover is not strictly necessary in the preparation of most dishes, but useful at times, especially for keeping food warm. You may not need to buy one—any pot lid of a diameter slightly less than that of the *wok* will do.

Metal ring-stands are often provided with *woks* sold in the U.S. It is often best to rest the *wok* directly on the burner

—the ring-stand just moves the *wok* further away from an already inadequate heat source. Keep the ring, however, for use in camping as you cook over a fire or coals with no grill.

Cleaning: Treat the *wok* as you would a good French omelette pan. Do not use detergents. Cylindrical *wok*-cleaners made from bamboo slivers bound at one end are available at Chinese grocery stores. They are preferable to nylon scouring pads because they can be used while the *wok* is still hot. Avoid using metal scouring pads. To clean, just run water into the *wok* and with the *wok*-cleaner or nylon pad loosen any food or grease adhering to the sides. Rinse, then replace on the fire and wipe out excess water with a rag if you are going to use *wok* immediately for preparing another dish. Heat for a few seconds to evaporate any remaining moisture before adding oil. Clean and wipe before storing.

Residual oil absorbed into the charred black layer which develops on the inside of the *wok* is what keeps food from sticking and the *wok* from rusting. If the *wok* does rust or if food does stick, scour the rust or foreign matter away, then wipe with a little oil and heat briefly. To season a new *wok*, scour thoroughly then heat ½ cup oil or so over low heat for about ½ hour, tilting the *wok* occasionally. Wipe and store.

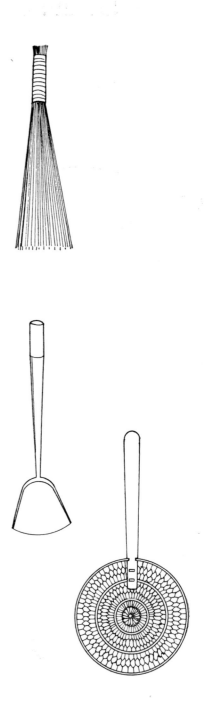

SPATULA/LADLE: Cooks in Chinese restaurants use a ladle to stir food. They keep oil, soy sauce, salt and various ingredients in pots in front of them and the ladle functions both as a stirrer and as a measuring and transferring device. At home, a shovel-shaped, wooden-handled utensil may work better. A wooden spatula or flat-bottomed spoon is excellent, because it is less likely to scratch the charred surface of the *wok*.

WIRE SPOON: The Chinese kind is made of twisted wire in various sizes from about 6-inches in diameter (the bowl of the spoon) and up. It is impossible to clean thoroughly, but it doesn't matter because the hot oil kill the "bad guys." A slotted spoon is a satisfactory substitute but is less efficient. An 8-inch wire scoop is a good thing for deep frying and it doubles for retrieving French fries too.

RICE COOKER: Optional equipment. Automatic and makes perfect rice every time. It does not take up a burner and it is easy to clean. You can leave the extra rice in it and reheat it with a little water the next day. Also doubles as a steamer and can be used for reheating things you don't want to fry.

OIL DRAINER: Optional. A colander will double, but if the holes are small, it is hard to clean.

The Chinese drainer is usually iron, shaped like a small, shallow *wok* with numerous holes about ½-inch apart. It should be placed over a medium-sized saucepan or a coffee can somewhere within easy reach of the stove. When you stir-fry vegetables, superior results can be obtained by using an excess of oil, thus making it possible to cook the vegetables very quickly. This is especially important if you are using an American stove—the inadequate heating power makes it advisable to use more oil because the introduction of the food tends to cool the oil faster than the flame can reheat it. After a few moments, the entire contents of the *wok* can be dumped into the oil drainer. This is much easier and faster than picking the food out with chopsticks or a wire spoon. Afterwards, the cooled oil that has collected in the bottom of the saucepan through the drainer can be reused. (For directions on how to reclaim oil, see page 30.)

CHINESE CLEAVER, or *Dao*: Absolutely essential. If you try to do all the chopping with a kitchen knife, it will take so long you'll never want to cook Chinese food again.

Buy a fairly heavy cleaver, wooden-handled if possible —one with a thick blade of carbon steel, not stainless. Stainless steel blades are almost impossible to sharpen once they lose their edge. The best size is one with about a 10-inch blade and about 4-inches high. Cleavers come in three weights: "big" (*da*, 大), "medium" (*chong*, 中) and "small" (*shao*, 小). The medium weight, or *chong*, is best for most purposes, but the big, or heavyweight, cleaver is good for cutting through light bones.

Buy a whetstone and use it occasionally. If you don't have one, try to find a curb made of fine concrete and use that. Hold the blade with both hands at about a 20-degree angle over the whetstone and with a circular motion sharpen the entire length of blade on both sides. Between sharpenings, the edge of the cleaver can be restored by running the blade across the chopping board at about a 45-degree angle, like a strap, using considerable force.

COOKING CHOPSTICKS: Nice looking when they get old and used. Sometimes convenient, but unnecessary.

CHOPPING BLOCK: Chinese cooks use a 6-inch thick round cut from a hardwood tree trunk. While these can be purchased at some Oriental provisions stores, any good cutting board will do. The surface should be wide enough to hold some volume of chopped ingredients, and it should be thick and heavy enough not to skate across the table while using the cleaver.

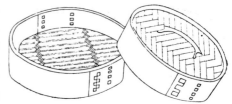

STEAMER: Bamboo steamers are sometimes available at Oriental provisions stores or at other specialty kitchenware stores. The advantage of the bamboo steamer is that less moisture forms on the inside of the lid during the steaming process. Arrange the food to be steamed in a flat heat-proof dish or foil pie pan before placing it in the steamer. Or if you are making any type of steamed bread, lightly grease the bamboo slats and then place the dough directly in the steamer.

An average-sized rice cooker can substitute for a steamer but is usually too small if you want to steam any quantity of food. It is easy to improvise a steamer by inverting several heat-proof cups in a large pot in an inch or more of water and placing a heat-proof plate over these. Cover with a tight-fitting lid (see figure at right). If quite a bit of moisture seems to be collecting on the bottom of the lid as the food steams, fold an absorbent dish towel and place it under the lid. Don't let the ends of the towel come anywhere near the flame.

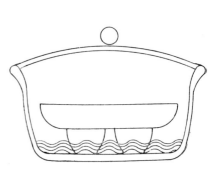

It is better to place the steamer over boiling water than to start steaming over cold water. Turn off the heat, take off the lid and let the steam disperse a bit before reaching in to remove steamed foods—or your fingers may be scalded.

METHODS

CHOPPING: THE BASIC IDEA

Chopping is undoubtedly the most formidable aspect of making Chinese food. In most cases chopping is 90% of the work and time that preparation involves, so learning to do it efficiently is the biggest hurdle in making Chinese food a feasible proposition instead of a half-day ordeal.

In general the following forms are required in Chinese cooking:

片	*pian*	slices	$\frac{1}{8}$ to $\frac{1}{4}$-inch thick, and 1 to 3-inches in length and width.
絲	*si*	shreds	$\frac{1}{8}$ to $\frac{1}{4}$-inch by $\frac{1}{4}$-inch, and 2 to 3-inches long.
末	*mo*	fine pieces	$\frac{1}{8}$-inch square or smaller.
丁	*ding*	chunks	$\frac{1}{2}$ to 1-inch cubes.

Fine pieces are most efficiently produced by cutting through a large number of shreds at one time, which in turn are similarly made from slices.

The Chinese cleaver, or *dao*, should be held well forward (see figure 1). Only the back three fingers and the heel of the palm are on the handle. For most operations, the forefinger extends down the outside of the back of the blade, with the thumb gripping the blade on the other side. Some cooks prefer to extend both the forefinger and the middle finger down the outside of the blade, leaving only two fingers on the handle. The front of the hand should be held over the back part of the blade of the cleaver, so that the heel or top of the blade rests slightly in front of the crease between the forefinger and palm.

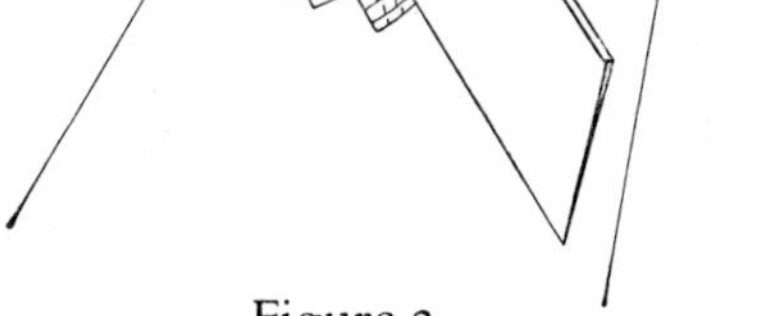

This grip may feel slightly strange at first, but it offers many advantages in terms of control and effort. Since the cleaver is usually used by rocking it with its tip resting on the chopping board as a fulcrum, it is possible to employ the weight of the cleaver to do much of the cutting. Most cutting

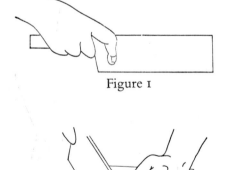

Figure 1

Figure 2

is done under the rear part of the blade, where leverage can be exercised most efficiently. The food to be cut is pushed through with the free hand, or the cleaver can be rotated in an arc, keeping the tip firmly placed, cutting through the food which is held steady with the free hand.

For fine work in particular, place the knuckles of the hand which is steadying the food against and touching the blade of the cleaver. If the fingertips are then kept slightly curled, there is no danger of an accident (see figure 2).

Practice chopping with a potato, in the following manner:

A. Slice a piece off of one side to provide a firm base for the potato to rest on. Cut it into $\frac{1}{8}$-inch slices, either pushing the potato through $\frac{1}{8}$-inch at a time with the free hand, or moving the cleaver slightly between each slice, rocking the cleaver up and down with the forward tip of the blade resting on the cutting board (see figure 3).

B. If shreds are desired, loosely stack the slices produced as in step A, then slide the top of the pile towards the hand which steadies the food, so that the slices are all roughly staggered like fanned playing cards. In this way, the food can be held quite firmly without bringing your fingers too close to the cleaver. Cut through the stack of slices again to produce shreds (see figure 4).

C. If fine pieces are desired, rotate the pile of shreds 90° and, holding the pile carefully, chop again. Very fine pieces can be produced by quickly chopping through the entire pile, this time picking up the cleaver and using the entire length of the blade with force (see figure 5).

NOTE: The cleaver should be as sharp as possible. Use a rag to wipe off the food which sticks to the blade between operations. The wide blade may also be used to scoop up whatever you have chopped to transfer to a plate or small bowl until it is needed.

MEAT: PORK, BEEF AND LAMB

Meat, being both soft and fibrous, is the most difficult thing to chop. The easy way out (a course adopted by many restaurants) is to freeze the meat first, after which it can be easily shaved into slices as thin as desired, as if it were the potato in the exercise above. Thaw slices completely before cooking.

If meat is unfrozen, the procedure is slightly different

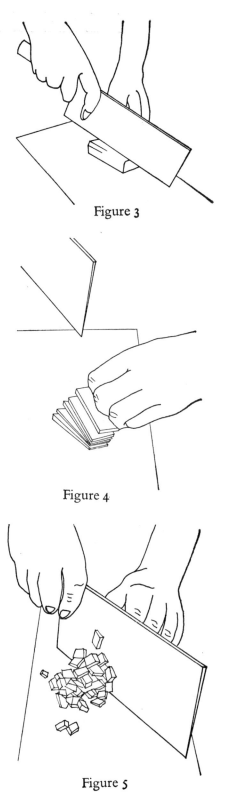

Figure 3

Figure 4

Figure 5

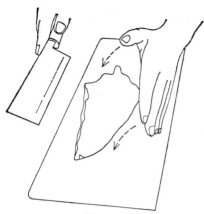

Figure 6

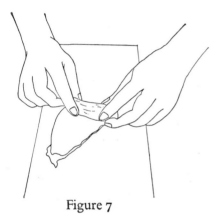

Figure 7

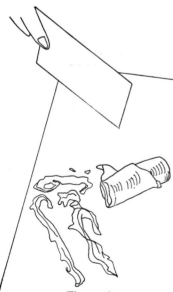

Figure 8

and slightly more difficult. The first series of slices is made parallel to the plane of the chopping board, with the hand on top of the meat, holding it as firmly as possible. Sandwiched between the hand and the chopping board, the meat will be semirigid. Pass the cleaver through as close to the chopping board as possible, moving the blade slowly with a slight sawing motion. Repeat this step until all the meat is sliced (see figure 6).

Shreds of meat may be made either in the manner indicated above (Step B), by piling the slices so that they overlap, or by rolling up each slice of meat and cutting "slices" from the roll, which will unravel into shreds when they are cooked (see figures 7 and 8). The meat should be cut across the grain, but with Western cuts this is often impossible.

Chicken breasts may be cut in this manner, or, if desired, you may simply hack them (bones and all) into chunks. (Boning chicken is treated separately below.) Most middle or heavyweight Chinese cleavers can be used to hack through chicken or light bones without damage to the blade, but lightweight or thin-blade cleavers may occasionally chip. If you intend to do this frequently, it is advisable to have a heavyweight, thick-bladed cleaver reserved exclusively for this purpose.

GINGER AND GARLIC:

Both these ingredients are used in such large quantities in Szechwanese cooking—frequently chopped as finely as possible—that they deserve special attention.

Fresh ginger seems to become more fibrous, and thus more difficult to chop, the older it gets. It is most economical to peel the ginger first (only as much as you intend to use), using a cleaver or paring knife to remove the peel from difficult-to-get-at corners. Make as regular a shape as possible (which can be wasteful) before proceeding further. Make the first series of cuts (into slices) through or across the grain of the ginger.

Garlic is a problem simply because the cloves are so small. Crush the peeled garlic slightly with the side of the cleaver to facilitate chopping. In most cases it is best to apply the general principle of "slice-to-shred-to-fine pieces" chopping as much as possible. Finely chopped garlic and ginger tend to dry out if left uncovered for any length of time—it is best to chop them within the hour they are to be used.

JOINTING A CHICKEN

Very often the most economical way of using a chicken is to buy a whole bird. Almost all of it can be used in some fashion or other. The following instructions (in connection with this, thanks to Mr. Kazō Satō and Mr. Akio Uzawa, proprietor and employee respectively of the Buroirā Satō poultry shop in Tokyo) assume only that the chicken in question is dead and that the feathers have been removed. With practice, the entire procedure of jointing should take no more than 4 or 5 minutes. A skilled butcher can turn a whole chicken into a plateful of boned chicken meat and a carcass and pile of bones in less than two minutes.

Use a freshly sharpened cleaver or a very sharp-pointed knife. Allow yourself enough room to work easily. Use a heavy chopping board.

A. To dismember the chicken, place the bird breast side up with the legs closest to you. Make fairly deep cuts parallel to the bird's breast through the skin and flesh on both sides where the legs join the body (see figure 9). Press the legs open.

B. Turn the chicken on its side, grasp the leg and pull it up and to the rear. Through the cut just made, sever the joint that should now be visible. Grasping the leg just above the cut, twist forcefully and pull the thigh and drumstick away, cutting as necessary (see figures 10 and 11). Turn the chicken and repeat. If the thigh and drumstick are not to be boned, cut the thigh from the drumstick at the joint and cut off and discard the lower leg and claws.

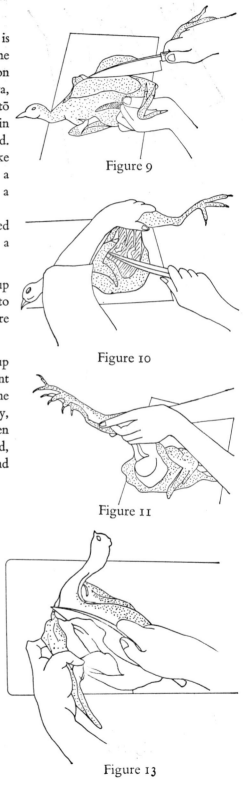

Figure 9

Figure 10

Figure 11

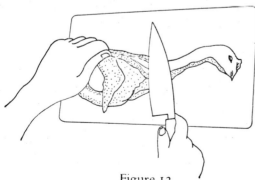

Figure 12

Figure 13

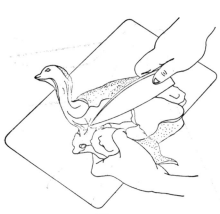

Figure 14

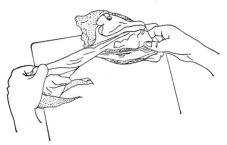

Figure 15

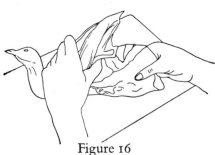

Figure 16

C. If the head and neck are still attached, place the chicken on its side, neck facing left if you are right-handed, or vice versa. Cut through the skin of the neck and down toward the body to release the flap of skin on the neck (see figure 12).

D. With the chicken still resting on its side, start at the side of the base of the neck and bring the cleaver or knife under the entire wing, cutting quite deeply. Make a parallel, deep cut on the opposite side of the flat bone that should now be visible near the joint that attaches the wing to the body (see figure 13 and 14). Grasp the entire wing firmly (and, if applicable, the flap of neck skin released in Step C, above) and pull the wing down toward the vent end of the bird, severing the large joint which attaches the wing to the body. Continue to pull down and toward the rear (see figure 15). The breast meat, except for the small inner fillets on either side of the breastbone and rib cage, will come away with the wing. When you have pulled the wing and breast meat away from the breast end of the body to the vent, cut through the skin and fat to free the wing and breast completely. Turn the chicken and repeat on the opposite side of the bird.

E. To release the breastbone and rib cage from the rest of the carcass, simply pull the former forward and up (see figure 16). The small fillets on either side of the rib cage may be removed by cutting through the tendons where they attach at the front of the breast and by pulling the meat away with your fingers. The tendon may be removed from the fillet by holding the larger tendon end against the chopping board with your free hand and scraping the meat away with the cleaver (see fingre 17).

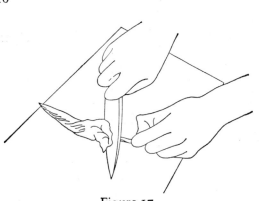

Figure 17

Figure 18

F. If the chicken has not been cleaned previously, remove the entrails at this point. Insert your hand into the cavity, pushing the entrails down toward the tail and out, severing the fatty tissue at the tail. Remove and save the heart and liver. Remove the kidneys and make a lateral cut almost all the way through from the thinnest edge. Spread it open and scrape away the yellow lining and cut away surrounding fatty tissue. Wash thoroughly in cold water. Discard the rest.

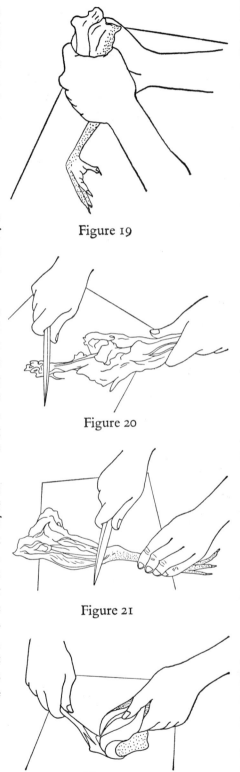

Figure 19

TO BONE DRUMSTICKS AND THIGHS

A. Place the chicken leg and thigh on the chopping board as shown, inside facing up. Starting just above the first joint of the drumstick, make a long and deep incision with the point of the cleaver or knife, following the bone the entire length to the end of the thigh (see figure 18).

B. Grasp the drumstick in one hand and the thigh in the other, with the incision facing up. Bend the drumstick and thigh straight down so that the joint between the drumstick and thigh is exposed (see figure 19). Then holding the bent drumstick and thigh in one hand, rest it on the chopping board with the thigh section directly on the board's surface and with the drumstick on the thigh. Sever the exposed joint. Hold the exposed thigh bone stationary on the chopping block with the cleaver as shown at right and pull away the thigh meat and drumstick (see figure 20).

Figure 20

C. Rest the drumstick and boned thigh on the chopping board, again with the inside facing up. Raise the cleaver or knife a few inches and bring it down sharply on the inside of the drumstick just above the first joint—hard enough to break the bone, but not hard enough to sever it (see figure 21). Turn the leg and boned thigh over and break the bone in the same place by cracking once sharply with the cleaver or knife. Picking up the leg, bend it in half at the first joint where you have just broken the bone. The broken end of the drumstick will protrude. Grasp the drumstick bone and remove, pulling toward the drumstick-thigh joint (see figure 22). Cut off and discard the claws, lower leg and first joint. If the claws and lower leg have been removed, cut away and discard the gristle and knuckle of the drumstick.

Figure 21

Figure 22

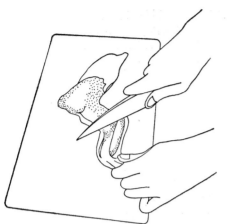

Figure 23

SEPARATING THE WING AND BREAST

A. Separate the wing at its middle joint, then cut the remaining wing at the joint that attaches it to the breast (see figure 23). You will be left with two wing pieces and half the chicken's breast.

B. Cut away the excess skin and fat of the breast, depending upon how you want to use this piece (see figure 24). To make small fillets, make a narrow incision along the sides of the breast meat and pull the fillets away from any remaining bone, cutting where necessary (see figure 25). Remove tendons as directed above (JOINTING A CHICKEN: Step E).

Figure 24

Figure 25

ORGANIZATION

Try to have ingredients as ready to go as possible before you begin cooking. Group together foods that will be added together so that nothing will be forgotten. Larger items, like cut vegetables, can be temporarily placed in the serving bowl—along with other ingredients that will be added and cooked *at the same time*.

Have the things you will need for almost every dish—salt, soy sauce, chopped garlic, chopped ginger, sesame oil, cornstarch, sugar, etc.—arrayed near the stove. Set an oil drainer near the burner. You will also need a small cup or bowl for making the cornstarch and water mixture that is so frequently used. (If you mix the cornstarch and water ahead of time, remember to give it a quick stir before adding it to the other ingredients in the *wok* because cornstarch tends to settle out of solution quickly). It is also handy to have a set of measuring spoons, a Chinese soup spoon or a large serving spoon and a pair of chopsticks and something to rest the sticky ladle or spatula on. You will need a dishcloth or clean rag.

If necessary, review the recipe before you begin to cook. Try to avoid having to consult it while you're cooking—just get an idea of what you're supposed to do. Outside of speed, few things are critical in Szechwanese cooking, not excepting specific measures. Chinese cookbooks often note the measures in general terms or omit them entirely. In writing the recipes for this book, I have given the measurements that I use, so "correct" these to your personal taste. In Chinese restaurants, cooks take quite a bit of liberty in varying measures and even the ingredients themselves. Feel free to do the same.

STIR-FRYING

Stir-frying is a technique commonly used in the preparation of Chinese foods. When a recipe notes that a few tablespoons of cooking oil are to be heated in the *wok* and that the ingredients are to be "stir-fried," "stir-cooked" or "tossed," I am referring to this technique.

You should make sure that the *wok* is dry before adding the oil. The best method is to heat the *wok* over the flame after wiping it out and before adding the oil. (If any moisture remains, the hot oil will spatter). Usually the best temperature for stir-frying is that obtained when the oil rolls freely in the *wok* if the *wok* is gently moved but before the oil begins to smoke. If the oil has started to smoke but not heavily, it is not necessary to allow the oil to cool before adding the ingredients. When the ingredients have been added, use a spatula, cooking chopsticks, or a wooden spoon to stir the pieces of food around, making sure they are evenly coated with oil and heated thoroughly.

OIL—TO USE AND REUSE

Peanut oil is preferred for deep frying and stir-frying because it can be heated to a high temperature without burning and can be used repeatedly without clarification, but any vegetable oil is perfectly satisfactory, for example, corn or safflower oil. For stir-frying you can substitute lard but never use butter (it will burn), olive oil (too heavy) or shortening (which congeals and spoils the texture of the food). Raw peanut oil, such as you can buy in health food stores, foams and will scorch.

The most efficient and economical way to save oil is to arrange an oil drainer (see page 21) near the cooking area—as handy to the burner as possible. When foods must be deep fried or stir-fried as a preliminary step in preparation, the entire contents of the *wok* may be emptied into the strainer. The cooked ingredients are thus out of the way until needed again, by which time they will be well drained of excess oil. The oil which collects in the saucepan can be filtered for reuse in the following manner.

To reclaim cooking oil, pass it through a strainer—either a fine wire one, cheesecloth, or even strong paper toweling. If you have cooked with inexpensive oil, pour the used oil into the *wok* or frying pan before straining. Add a slice or two of fresh ginger and a green onion cut into 1-inch sections and let the ginger and green onion brown over medium heat. Remove and discard these and allow the oil to cool. This step is rarely necessary with peanut oil. Finally, strain and store, unrefrigerated, in a sealed container.

SERVING SUGGESTIONS

There are no real rules for the selection of dishes beyond the dictates of common sense. You should avoid monotony by not making dishes which have the same seasonings and sauces. And you should—particularly if you are having guests—provide alternatives to hot or highly spiced dishes. Thus, don't serve two yu-xiang sauce dishes such as Eggplant with Yu-xiang Sauce and Pork Liver with Yu-xiang Sauce. On the other hand, Eggplant with Yu-xiang Sauce and *Ma-po Dou-fu* go well together since the *dou-fu* dish is hot and gingery while the yu-xiang dish stresses garlic and somewhat underplays the hotness of the former. A *ma-la*, or "peppery and hot," dish or Chengtu Chicken, for example, could be served with these since it emphasizes the flavor of black or Szechwan pepper. Still another alternative would be to serve a dish calling for fresh or dried red peppers. There is no need to worry about serving more than one or two chicken dishes at one meal—the flavorings and sauces will be different. And, with other kinds of meat becoming more expensive, chicken as a main dish is convenient because it can be prepared in any number of ways.

It is difficult to say how many persons one Chinese dish will serve, but if you are preparing a Chinese-style meal where everyone helps himself from the serving dishes and samples all that is offered, one dish per person is a good principle to follow. So, four dishes will serve four people, and so on. The recipes in the following pages will serve 1–2 persons at a Chinese-style meal, but if served as a side-dish in a Western-style meal, they will feed as many as 4 or 5. To cook Chinese doesn't mean that everything you prepare for a meal must be Chinese. To experiment and to learn how to prepare Chinese dishes, start by serving single dishes along with other Western foods. Chinese food need not be served with white rice—serve it with brown rice or bread, if that is your favorite.

To the question of the order in which dishes should be served, the only point of consequence is that in China soups are served last, for they help settle a meal and complete it. The advantage of this custom will be obvious once you have tried it a few times. With a few exceptions, it doesn't matter whether you serve the more delicately flavored dishes first and the hotter, more highly spiced dishes last, or vary the order of serving.

Set the table with knife and fork, and a soup spoon if there is a soup course. You will notice, however, that Chinese foods generally come to the table in bite-sized pieces, and carving or cutting at table is the exception rather than the rule. Try using chopsticks—they are not difficult to use if you hold them in a relaxed but firm manner. Three-fourths of the way up the shaft, cradle the chopsticks on the side of your first knuckle and encircle the chopsticks with thumb and forefinger. The bottom chopstick should remain stationary at all times and rests on the tip of your ring finger. The upper chopstick, which moves in a pincerlike motion against the lower chopstick, rests between the tips of your forefinger and middle finger. Follow these directions or devise your own method of handling chopsticks.

As to the best beverage to drink with a Szechwan-style meal, I'm convinced that nothing is better than beer and I invariably serve or order beer with a Szechwanese meal. Tea, in my opinion, is something to drink before or after a meal, not with it—but that is a matter of taste. If you want to serve wine, I would suggest a dry red, powerful enough to stand up to the garlic and peppers—which is asking a lot of any wine. Chinese wines from the People's Republic of China and from Taiwan are now becoming more and more available in the United States, though few Americans are truly fond of them. If you do serve Chinese wine or Japanese saké, warm it first by placing it in a heat-proof container or decanter and lowering it into a simmering hot-water bath. If you place the entire commercial bottle in the hot-water bath, crack open the top first. The stronger Chinese beverages such as *mao-tai* and *gao-liang* (color: page 40) are not really wines at all—some varieties of *gao-liang* are as powerful as 180 proof. Most of these beverages should be heated as directed above. Serve in tiny wine cups and treat with respect.

1. Fresh bamboo shoot
2. and 5. Hot bean sauce
3. Sesame paste
4. Sesame oil
6. Chinese cabbage
7. Green onions
8. Winter melon
9. Dried mushrooms
10. Eggplants
11. Canned bamboo shoot
12. Green peppers
13. Transparent vermicelli
14. Fresh ginger
15. Fresh garlic cloves
16. Snow peas
17. Fresh mushrooms
18. Canned water chestnuts
19. Dried red peppers
20. Cashews
21. Fresh noodles
22. *Dou-fu,* or bean curd
23. Sweet bean sauce
24. Szechwan vegetable
25. Star anise
26. Dried orange peel
27. Fermented black beans
28. Wood ear
29. Dried shrimps
30. Szechwan pepper
31. Straw mushrooms
32. Dried scallops

33

Clockwise: Steamed Bread (p. 106), Dry-fried Beef with Carrots and Celery (p. 61), Crispy-skin Chicken (p. 52), Braised Eel with Bamboo Shoot (p. 84), Hot and Sour Soup (p. 104)

34

Chicken with Red Pepper Shreds (p. 49), "Ants Climbing a Tree"—Transparent Vermicelli with Pork and Hot Bean Sauce (p. 108), Eggplant with Yu-xiang Sauce (p. 93)

"Lions' Heads"—Szechwan-style Meatballs (p. 66), Chengtu Chicken (p. 48), Twice-cooked Pork (p. 68)

Clockwise: Red Snapper prepared in the manner of Western-Lake Sour Fish (p. 80), Flash-cooked Duck Pieces (p. 56), Dry-fried String Beans (p. 95), Chicken with Dried Orange Peel and Red Peppers (p. 46), Szechwan-vegetable and Pork-shred Soup (p. 103), Fresh Fruit Dessert

Chicken with Charred Red Peppers and Cashews (p. 45),
Ma-po Dou-fu (p. 96), Flash-fried Lamb with Green Onion (p. 60)

RECIPES

POULTRY

In many parts of Asia, unlike the West, poultry, especially chicken, has been the most prized of meats and often the most expensive. Modern methods of mass-producing fryers in a very short period of time are changing this situation. However, in Taiwan where these techniques have penetrated, a distinction is made between birds which have been raised naturally, with no special foods and a normal amount of exercise, and the new breeds of chicken which are tightly confined in cages and given growth-accelerating drugs and feed. The meat of the former is of course tougher—it is also said to be tastier. Duck is a relatively common and inexpensive food in China, especially in areas of rice agriculture, where ducks can be raised with little or no extra commitment of land or feed.

The methods of preparation for both duck and chicken are similar, with consideration given to the higher fat content of duck. Thus both duck and chicken are commonly fried, or steamed and fried. However, duck is never simply boiled, while chicken is. Roasting, as in the famous Peking Duck recipe, is a fairly recent import from Central Asia.

The most practical way to buy chicken is whole. It can then be jointed and boned according to the instructions on page 26. Of the pieces sold in American markets, breasts are the easiest to bone and most recipes in this section have been given in terms of breast meat. Rather than using boneless meat, you may also use other cuts and simply hack through chicken pieces, bone and all. Pieces cut in this way should be allowed slightly more time to cook.

Ma-la Zi Ji
PEPPERY AND HOT CHICKEN

麻辣子鷄

Ma-la Zi Ji *is fairly hot, quite spicy and also has a peppery flavor.*

1 whole chicken breast, about 1
   lb. when boned
MARINADE
   1 Tbsp. cornstarch
   1 Tbsp. rice wine or dry
   sherry
   1 egg white

TO PREPARE: 1. Bone the chicken breast (see page 29) and cut the meat into 1-inch pieces, or slightly smaller. Make the MARINADE by mixing the cornstarch with the wine and then beating in the egg white. Mix with the chicken and marinate at least 15 minutes.

2. Slice the water chestnuts thinly. Chop the green onion coarsely and the ginger and garlic finely.

4–6 water chestnuts
4–5 Tbsps. chopped green onion
1–2 Tbsps. finely chopped fresh
　ginger
1–2 Tbsps. finely chopped garlic
1 Tbsp. hot bean sauce
SEASONINGS
　　2 tsps. cornstarch
　　1 Tbsp. chicken stock or
　　water
　　1 Tbsp. soy sauce
　　2 tsps. sugar
　　1 tsp. vinegar
　　2 tsps. sesame oil
　　1 tsp. ground Szechwan
　　pepper
　　$\frac{1}{2}$ tsp. black pepper
　　1 tsp. salt
approximately $\frac{1}{2}$ cup oil

3. To make the SEASONINGS, first mix the cornstarch with the stock or water and soy sauce in a small bowl, then add and mix the remaining SEASONINGS ingredients.

To COOK: 1. Heat $\frac{1}{4}$ cup of the cooking oil or slightly more in a *wok* or large frying pan until very hot. Pour extra MARINADE off the chicken and add the chicken pieces to the heated oil. Stir to keep the pieces separate as they cook. (It may be necessary to cook the chicken a few pieces at a time if your heat source is insufficient to cook all the chicken quickly and at once.) When the chicken has turned white, remove and drain.

2. Leave only 3 Tbsps. or so cooking oil in the *wok*. Heat this oil and add the hot bean sauce, green onion, ginger and garlic. Stir together over a high heat until the garlic and ginger begin to absorb the red color from the hot bean sauce. Return the prefried chicken pieces and add the water chestnuts and SEASONINGS (give it a quick stir first). Stir, checking for salt. When the chicken is reheated and the sauce has thickened slightly, remove to a serving dish and serve hot.

Gan-shao Ji-kuai
BRAISED CHICKEN PIECES

乾燒鷄塊

$\frac{1}{2}$ lb. chicken breast
$\frac{1}{4}$ cup bamboo shoot
3–4 dried mushrooms
SEASONINGS
　　1 tsp. finely chopped green
　　onion
　　1 tsp. finely chopped fresh
　　ginger
　　1 tsp. cornstarch mixed
　　with 2 tsps. water
　　1 Tbsp. rice wine or dry
　　sherry
　　1 tsp. soy sauce
　　1 tsp. salt
　　1 tsp. sugar
　　2 cups chicken stock
2 tsps. cornstarch mixed with 4
tsps. water
4–6 Tbsps. oil

To PREPARE: 1. Clean the chicken and cut the meat into 1-inch bite-sized pieces.

2. Cut the bamboo shoot into thick, bite-sized pieces. Soak the dried mushrooms in warm water until softened, cut away tough stems, and quarter. Chop the green onion and ginger finely.

3. Mix the SEASONINGS in a cup or small bowl, first mixing the cornstarch in the water, adding the wine and soy sauce next and then stirring in the other ingredients. Mix well.

To COOK: 1. Heat 4–6 Tbsps. cooking oil in a *wok* or large frying pan until very hot. Add the chicken pieces and stir-fry for about 30 seconds, or until the chicken becomes white. Then add the bamboo shoot and mushrooms. Stir well.

2. Stir and add the SEASONINGS. Reduce heat and simmer 8–10 minutes. When the liquid has been reduced to almost nothing, mix the 2 tsps. cornstarch with the water, and then add it a little at a time, stirring the dish all the while. The sauce will soon thicken and adhere to the chicken pieces. Remove from heat, transfer to a serving dish, and serve hot.

Sui-mi Ji

碎米鷄

CHICKEN WITH PEANUTS, CABBAGE AND RED PEPPERS

Sui-mi Ji is slightly hot and the crushed peanuts give it an unusual flavor. This dish reheats well and leftovers make a good base for fried rice.

1 whole chicken breast, about 1 lb. when boned

MARINADE

    1 Tbsp. cornstarch

    1 Tbsp. rice wine or dry sherry

    1 Tbsp. soy sauce

    1/2 tsp. salt

1/2 cup crushed peanuts (if salted peanuts are used, reduce or omit the salt from the SEASONINGS)

3–4 fresh or dried red peppers

1/4 head round cabbage

2–3 Tbsps. chopped green onion

1 Tbsp. finely chopped fresh ginger

1 Tbsp. finely chopped garlic (optional)

1 Tbsp. hot bean sauce

SEASONINGS

    1 Tbsp. cornstarch

    1 Tbsp. rice wine or dry sherry

    2 Tbsps. soy sauce

    1 1/2–2 tsps. salt (reduce or omit if salted peanuts are used)

    1 tsp. vinegar

    1 tsp. sugar

    2 tsps. sesame oil

approximately 2/3 cup oil

TO PREPARE: 1. Bone the chicken breast (see page 29) and cut the meat into small 1/2 or 3/4-inch pieces. Make the MARINADE by mixing the cornstarch with the wine and soy sauce and then adding the salt. Mix with the chicken and marinate at least 15 minutes.

2. Crush the peanuts with the side of the cleaver, pressing down on the horizontal blade with the heel of your palm, or chop them. The peanuts should be reduced to the size of grains of rice but should not be powdered.

3. Cut the fresh or dried red peppers in half lengthwise and remove seeds with the tip of a knife. Cut the peppers into slivers. Set aside together with the peanuts.

4. Chop the ginger and garlic finely and the green onion coarsely. Core the cabbage and cut it into pieces about 1-inch by 1-inch.

5. Mix the SEASONINGS, first mixing the cornstarch with the wine and vinegar, then adding the other ingredients.

TO COOK: 1. Heat 6 Tbsps. of the cooking oil in a *wok* or large frying pan until very hot. Add the cabbage and a pinch of salt and stir-fry very quickly. Remove and drain when the cabbage starts to soften and looks slightly cooked. Arrange the cabbage on both ends of a serving platter leaving a space in the center.

2. Heat 4–5 Tbsps. of the cooking oil in the *wok* until very hot. Add the chicken pieces and cook quickly. (If necessary use more oil and drain later, or cook the chicken a few pieces at a time.) When the chicken is white, add the ginger, garlic, green onion, peanuts and red peppers. Stir briefly, then add the hot bean sauce. Cook, stirring, for another 10–15 seconds, or until the hot bean sauce is well distributed and you can smell the ginger and hot bean sauce. Then stir the SEASONINGS and add them to the *wok*. Cook for a few more seconds, stirring, then remove the contents of the *wok* to the center of the serving dish between the piles of fried cabbage. Serve hot.

An alternate method of cooking is to use slightly less pre-fried cabbage and to add it after the hot bean sauce but before the SEASONINGS.

Gong-bao Ji-ding

公保鷄丁

CHICKEN WITH CHARRED RED PEPPERS AND CASHEWS

COLOR: page 40

The story is that when a certain Ting Kung-pao of Kweichow received an appointment as an imperial official to Szechwan, he prepared a dinner for his friends that included this dish, which then took his name. Gong-bao Ji-ding, in one form or another, is one of the best known and most often prepared Szechwanese foods, especially outside China. Whole dried red peppers are purposely cooked until they are burnt, flavoring the oil in which the chicken is to be cooked. The final dish should be somewhat sweet and slightly spicy and also hot from the charred red peppers of which there should be an adequate supply. Many restaurants skimp on the red peppers and add red oil and the result is a dull Gong-bao Ji-ding. Be careful when you cook this dish because the volatile oil of red peppers tends to be released into the air while the peppers are cooking. If you don't have a hood and fan over your stove, open all the windows and keep doors to other rooms closed while charring the peppers.

½ chicken breast, about ½ lb.
    when boned

MARINADE

    2 tsps. cornstarch

    2 tsps. soy sauce

    1 Tbsp. rice wine or dry
    sherry

    ½–1 egg white

    ½ tsp. salt

10 dried red peppers, or a few
    more

2 tsps. finely chopped fresh
    ginger

1 green onion

¼ cup cashews, or peanuts or
    almonds

SEASONINGS

    2 tsps. cornstarch

    2 tsps. rice wine or dry
    sherry

    1–2 Tbsps. soy sauce

    1 tsp. vinegar

    ½ tsp. salt (omit if using
    salted nuts)

    1–2 tsps. sugar

    2 tsps. sesame oil (optional
    —in this dish I prefer omit-
    ting the sesame oil)

4 Tbsps. oil

TO PREPARE: 1. Bone the chicken breast (see page 29) and cut the meat into pieces, 1-inch or slightly smaller.

2. Make the MARINADE by mixing the cornstarch with 2 tsps. soy sauce and 1 Tbsp. wine, then adding the salt and egg white. Mix the MARINADE with the chicken and marinate at least 15 minutes.

3. Cut off the ends of the dried red peppers and shake out the seeds. Chop the ginger very finely and cut the green onion into ¾-inch lengths.

4. In a small bowl, mix the SEASONINGS, first mixing the cornstarch with the soy sauce and wine and then mixing in the other ingredients.

TO COOK: 1. Heat about 4 Tbsps. cooking oil in a *wok* or large frying pan. Add the red peppers, cooking over a medium flame until they start to char. Turn the fire up as high as possible and as soon as the peppers are black, add the chicken pieces. Reduce flame to medium.

2. Stir-fry until the chicken is white, then add the ginger and green onion. Cook, stirring for a few more seconds, then add the cashews or other nuts and the SEASONINGS (give it a quick stir first). When the sauce has thickened slightly and is glaze-like, remove to a serving dish and serve hot.

Ban-ban Ji

棒棒鷄

COLD CHICKEN WITH SESAME AND SPICE SAUCE

This is a good warm-weather dish. It can be served either as an appetizer or as a regular course. A major advantage is that everything is simple and can be done ahead of time. Since the chicken is to be cut into shreds after boiling, you can economize and buy a whole small chicken or even chicken legs instead of the more expensive chicken breasts.

1 whole chicken breast
SEASONINGS (per lb. of meat)
    2–3 Tbsps. finely chopped
    fresh ginger
    2–3 Tbsps. finely chopped
    garlic
    4–6 Tbsps. sesame paste
    4–6 Tbsps. red oil
    2 tsps. Chinese red vinegar
    or white vinegar
    2–3 Tbsps. soy sauce
    1–2 Tbsps. sugar
    $\frac{1}{2}$ tsp. ground Szechwan
    pepper
    2–3 Tbsps. sesame oil

TO PREPARE AND COOK: 1. Clean the chicken and place it in enough boiling water to cover in a *wok* or pot. Boil until tender. It will take from 10–30 minutes depending on whether you are using breasts, legs, or a whole small chicken. Remove and drain. When cool, bone the chicken and cut its meat into shreds, about $\frac{3}{4}$-inch thick, $\frac{1}{4}$-inch wide (or smaller) and about 1-inch long. Arrange on a serving plate (on a bed of some decorative, leafy-type vegetable if you are feeling aesthetic).
2. While the chicken is boiling, chop the ginger and garlic finely. Mix the SEASONINGS in a small bowl.
3. Just before the dish is to be served, pour the SEASONINGS over the chicken shreds. Serve at room temperature.

Chen-pi Ji

陳皮鷄

CHICKEN WITH DRIED ORANGE PEEL AND RED PEPPERS
COLOR: page 38

Chen-pi Ji should be served at room temperature as an appetizer or as a cold main dish. Its taste is slightly hot.

$\frac{1}{2}$ chicken breast, about $\frac{1}{2}$ lb.
    when boned
2–3 pieces dried orange peel
2 dried red peppers
1 slice fresh ginger
1 green onion
2 tsps. sesame oil
1 tsp. salt
$\frac{1}{2}$ tsp. ground Szechwan pepper
$\frac{1}{2}$ tsp. sugar
2 Tbsps. soy sauce

TO PREPARE: Bone the chicken breast (see page 29) and cut the meat into bite-sized pieces. Soak the dried orange peels in warm water to soften before cutting the peels into slivers. Cut off the ends of the dried red peppers and shake out the seeds. If desired, cut the red peppers into slivers. (If you do, the dish will be hotter.) Slice the ginger into slivers and cut the green onion into 1-inch lengths.

TO COOK: 1. Heat 2 Tbsps. cooking oil in a *wok* or large frying pan. Add the sesame oil and salt. Add the chicken pieces and stir-fry over medium heat until the liquid disappears and

46

1 tsp. rice wine or dry sherry
½–1 tsp. red oil
2 Tbsps. oil

the smell of cooked chicken is noticeable. Keep the chicken from sticking to the *wok* by stirring constantly.

2. Reduce the heat, and add the orange peels, red peppers, Szechwan pepper, wine, sugar, soy sauce, ginger and green onion and red oil. Cook over low heat for 10 minutes, then increase heat to medium or high. Continue to cook for another minute or so, or until the liquid has thickened and has been reduced somewhat. Check for salt and then arrange on a serving dish and allow to cool or chill. If the chicken becomes dry while cooling, sprinkle lightly with soy sauce just before serving. A few drops of sesame oil may also be added just before serving.

Jiao-ma Ji-pian

椒麻鷄片

COLD CHICKEN SLICES WITH SESAME AND SZECHWAN PEPPER

Jiao-ma Ji-pian is very similar to Cold Chicken with Red Oil Sauce (see page 50) and Cold Chicken with Sesame and Spice Sauce (see page 46), but in this dish the sauce is simpler, emphasizing sesame and Szechwan pepper taste and the chicken is cut into slices. If you don't slice the chicken, drop the word pian, *or "slice," from the recipe's Chinese name. Very simple, very good, serve as a cold dish or as an appetizer.*

1 whole small chicken*
SEASONINGS (per lb. of meat)
    2 Tbsps. finely chopped green onion (optional)
    2 Tbsps. finely chopped fresh ginger
    3 Tbsps. soy sauce
    2 tsps. vinegar
    2 Tbsps. sesame oil
    1 tsp. salt
    1 tsp. ground Szechwan pepper
    1 tsp. sugar

*Chicken breast may also be used as breast meat is easily cut into neat slices.

TO PREPARE AND COOK: 1. Clean the chicken and place it in enough boiling water in a *wok* or pot so that the chicken is covered. Boil until tender but not overdone. Remove, drain and allow to cool. When the chicken has cooled, cut the meat into thin slices and arrange attractively on a serving platter.

2. Chop the green onion and ginger finely. Then mix the SEASONINGS in a small bowl.

3. To serve, pour the SEASONINGS over the chicken slices and garnish with parsley. Serve at room temperature.

Cheng-du Ji

CHENGTU CHICKEN

COLOR: page 37

成 都 鷄

Chengtu is the present capital of Szechwan. Strictly speaking, Cheng-du Ji should be prepared using only chicken, but it has become common practice to add bamboo shoot and tomatoes.

1 whole chicken breast, about
    1 lb. when boned
MARINADE
    1 Tbsp. cornstarch
    $1\frac{1}{2}$ Tbsps. rice wine or dry
    sherry
    $1\frac{1}{2}$ Tbsps. soy sauce
1–2 green onions
$\frac{1}{2}$–1 cup bamboo shoot
$\frac{1}{2}$ large (or 1 small) tomato
1 Tbsp. chopped fresh ginger
1 Tbsp. chopped garlic
1 Tbsp. hot bean sauce
SEASONINGS
    2 Tbsps. cornstarch
    $1\frac{1}{2}$ Tbsps. soy sauce
    1 tsp. vinegar
    1 tsp. sugar
    $\frac{1}{2}$–1 tsp. salt
    2 tsps. sesame oil
    $\frac{1}{2}$ tsp. ground Szechwan
    pepper
    1 Tbsp. ketchup (optional)
approximately $\frac{3}{4}$ cup oil

TO PREPARE: 1. Bone the chicken breast (see page 29) and cut the meat into $1\frac{1}{2}$-inch pieces. Mix the MARINADE and mix with the chicken and marinate at least 10 minutes.

2. Cut the green onion into 1-inch lengths. Cut the bamboo shoot into thin slices about $\frac{2}{3}$-inch wide, $\frac{1}{8}$-inch thick and 1-inch long. Stem and halve the tomato, and cut into thin wedges. Chop the ginger and garlic rather finely.

3. In a bowl, mix the SEASONINGS, first mixing the cornstarch with the soy sauce and vinegar, adding sugar, salt and finally mixing in the sesame oil, ground Szechwan pepper and ketchup.

TO COOK: 1. Heat about $\frac{2}{3}$ cup of the cooking oil in a *wok* or large frying pan until very hot. Add the chicken cubes and stir-fry until the chicken is white. Remove and drain. (If the heat source is inadequate, it may be preferable to cook the chicken a few pieces at a time, removing the cubes as they turn white.)

2. Heat 2 Tbsps. of the cooking oil in the *wok* and stir-fry the bamboo shoot briefly. Remove and drain.

3. Heat 3 Tbsps. of the cooking oil in the *wok* until very hot. Add the hot bean sauce, ginger, garlic and green onion. Stir-cook until you notice a distinct spicy smell and the ginger and garlic have absorbed the red color from the hot bean sauce. Add the prefried chicken and bamboo shoot. Stir briefly until everything is well mixed and heated. Then give the SEASON-INGS a stir and add along with the tomato wedges. Stir briefly and let the tomatoes heat through. Check for salt and remove to a serving dish. Serve hot.

Zuo Zong-tang Ji *or* La-jiao Zi Ji
左宗棠鷄

CHICKEN WITH RED PEPPER SHREDS

COLOR: page 36

Tso Tsung-t'ang whose name is included in this dish was a regional leader of Szechwan during the T'ung-chih Restoration (1862–1874). His role in the supression of the Nien (1853–1868) and Northwest Moslem (1862–1873) rebellions has made him an extremely unpopular figure in the People's Republic of China. So there as in Hong Kong, this dish is known as La-jiao Zi Ji, which means "Chicken with Red Peppers." Whichever name you decide to use, this is an impressive-looking dish, and it is suprisingly delicate in flavor. Be careful not to use too much egg white in the marinade or there will be extraneous pieces of fried egg as a result. The egg white marinade should just coat the chicken pieces. Be careful not to char the peppers when stir-frying—in this dish they are supposed to be bright red and only lightly cooked.

1 whole chicken breast, about 2½ to 3 cups when boned and cut into pieces

MARINADE
    2 tsps. cornstarch
    2 tsps. soy sauce
    ½ egg white
    ½ tsp. salt
4–6 fresh or dried red peppers
2 tsps. finely chopped fresh ginger
2 tsps. finely chopped garlic

SEASONINGS
    2 tsps. cornstarch
    1 Tbsp. rice wine or dry sherry
    1 Tbsp. soy sauce
    2 tsps. vinegar
    2 tsps. sesame oil
approximately 1 cup oil

TO PREPARE: 1. Bone the chicken breast (see page 29) and cut the meat into large cubes, 1-inch at most. Make MARINADE by mixing 2 tsps. cornstarch with 2 tsps. soy sauce and then adding the egg white and ½ tsp. salt. Mix MARINADE with chicken and marinate at least 10 minutes.

2. Cut the red peppers in half lengthwise, remove seeds with the tip of a knife and cut the peppers into thin strips about 1-inch long and ¼-inch wide. If you are using dried red peppers, soak them in warm water to soften and then proceed with directions as if the dried red peppers were fresh.

3. Chop the ginger and garlic as finely as possible.

4. Mix the SEASONINGS in a cup or small bowl, first mixing the cornstarch with the wine, then adding the other ingredients.

TO COOK: 1. Heat about 1 cup cooking oil in a *wok* or large frying pan until very hot. Pour the excess MARINADE off the chicken and add the meat to the oil and stir-fry for about 30 seconds, or until the chicken is white. Remove and drain.

2. Remove extra oil, leaving only 3 Tbsps. oil in the *wok*. Reheat this oil until it is very hot, then add the red pepper slivers and chopped ginger and garlic. When you notice the aroma of the garlic and ginger (probably 10–15 seconds), add the prefried chicken pieces. Stir the SEASONINGS and add them to the *wok*. Stir and when everything is well mixed, remove to a serving bowl and serve hot.

Hong-you Ji

紅油鷄

COLD CHICKEN WITH RED OIL SAUCE

Hong-you Ji may be served as an appetizer or as the first course of a meal. Easy to make and particularly appropriate for warm weather. Somewhat hot.

1 whole small chicken
SEASONINGS (per lb. of meat)
    2 Tbsps. finely chopped green onion
    2 Tbsps. finely chopped fresh ginger
    1/3 cup crushed peanuts (optional)
    2–3 Tbsps. red oil
    3 Tbsps. soy sauce
    1 Tbsp. vinegar
    2 Tbsps. sesame oil
    1 Tbsp. sesame paste (optional)
    1–2 tsps. sugar
    1/2 tsp. ground Szechwan pepper

TO PREPARE AND COOK: 1. Clean the chicken and place it in enough boiling water in a *wok* or pot so that the chicken is covered. Boil until tender but not overdone. Remove, drain and allow to cool. When the chicken has cooled, cut the meat off the bones, slice into bite-sized pieces and arrange attractively on a serving platter.
2. Chop the green onion and ginger finely. If peanuts are to be used, crush them with the slide of a cleaver or chop them coarsely. They should be about the size of grains of rice, not powdered. Then mix the SEASONINGS in a small bowl.
3. To serve, pour the SEASONINGS over the chicken pieces, garnish with parsley and serve at room temperature.

Dou-ya Qing-jiao Ji-si

豆芽青椒鷄絲

CHICKEN SHREDS WITH BEAN SPROUTS AND GREEN PEPPER

This is not really Szechwanese cooking. If anything, it's probably more typical of Shanghai or eastern cooking styles. It may be best to serve this dish, not at all hot or spicy, before serving highly-spiced entrees—otherwise its mild taste will be overpowered.

1 whole chicken breast, boned and shredded
MARINADE
    1 Tbsp. cornstarch
    1 Tbsp. rice wine or dry sherry
    2 egg whites
1/2 lb. bean sprouts

TO PREPARE: 1. Bone the chicken breast (see page 29) and cut the fillets in half to make thin but wide slices. Cut the chicken slices into shreds about 1/4-inch wide, 1/4-inch thick and 1 1/2-inches long. In a *wok* or pot, bring a quart of water (or more) to boil. Submerge the chicken in the boiling water just long enough for the shreds to turn white. Remove immediately and drain. Discard water.
2. MIX MARINADE, first mixing the cornstarch with the wine

2–3 green peppers, depending on size

SEASONINGS

    1 Tbsp. rice wine or dry sherry

    2 tsps. salt

    1 Tbsp. sesame oil

⅔ cup oil

and then stirring in the egg whites. Mix the MARINADE with the boiled chicken.

3. Wash the bean sprout thoroughly and remove their dark ends. Top and seed the peppers and cut them into shreds about the same size as the chicken shreds.

4. Mix the SEASONINGS in a small bowl.

TO COOK: 1. Heat ¼ cup of the cooking oil in a *wok* or large frying pan until very hot. Add the green pepper and stir-fry quickly, adding a pinch of salt. Remove and drain.

2. Heat another ¼ cup of the cooking oil in the *wok* until very hot and add the chicken shreds. Stir-fry quickly, using chopsticks to keep the pieces of chicken separate. Remove and drain.

3. Heat 3 Tbsps. of the cooking oil in the *wok* and add bean sprouts. Stir-fry quickly. As soon as the bean sprouts are covered with oil and heated, add the prefried chicken shreds and prefried green pepper. Add SEASONINGS. Stir briefly, remove to a serving dish and serve hot.

Guai-wei Ji

怪味鷄

"*STRANGE–TASTE*" *CHICKEN*

Guai-wei, or "strange taste," in the name of this dish refers to the flavors of sweetness, sourness, hotness, saltiness and spiciness that are all blended with no single flavor predominating. Since the strength of the various ingredients varies, the measures below may have to be adjusted slightly. If the taste of any ingredient is noticeably stronger than that of any other, reduce the amount of that ingredient a little the next time. Serve at room temperature.

1 whole small chicken

SEASONINGS (per lb. of meat)

    4 tsps. finely chopped fresh ginger

    2 Tbsps. finely chopped green onion

    4 tsps. finely chopped garlic

    4 tsps. sesame paste

    2 Tbsps. soy sauce

    4 tsps. red oil

    4 tsps. vinegar

    4 tsps. sesame oil

    2 tsps. sugar

    1 tsp. Szechwan pepper

TO COOK AND SERVE: 1. Place the whole chicken in a *wok* or pot in enough boiling water to cover. Boil until tender but not overdone. Remove and drain. When cool cut the meat into bite-sized pieces. Arrange attractively on a platter.

2. Chop the ginger, green onion and garlic finely and then mix all the SEASONINGS ingredients in a small bowl. Mix well.

3. Pour the SEASONINGS over the pieces of cooled chicken. Garnish with parsley. Serve at room temperature.

NOTE: If you add 2 or 3 thin slices of fresh ginger, 2 green onions cut into 3-inch lengths and 10–12 Szechwan peppercorns to the water in which the chicken is to boil, you may omit the ginger and ground Szechwan pepper (but not the chopped green onion) from the SEASONINGS.

Cui-pi Ji

脆 皮 鷄

CRISPY–SKIN CHICKEN
COLOR: page 35

This is not at all difficult to prepare although you do have to start thinking about making it a bit ahead of time. Parboiled, then glazed in honey and vinegar and deep fried, this chicken dish may become one of your favorites. I have given two lists of ingredients to use in the parboiling of the chicken—choose either one or make up one of your own.

1 whole small chicken, or ½ split chicken

PARBOILING INGREDIENTS A

    2 green onions, cut into 3-inch lengths

    2–3 slices fresh ginger, about ¼-inch thick

    1 small tomato, stemmed and quartered

    1 tsp. rice wine or dry sherry

    1 Tbsp. salt

    1 tsp. sugar

    1 tsp. ground Szechwan pepper

    ½ tsp. five spices, or a small sliver of fresh orange peel

PARBOILING INGREDIENTS B

    1 tsp. rice wine or dry sherry

    1 Tbsp. salt

    1 tsp. ground Szechwan pepper

    3 pieces star anise

    1 piece dried orange peel, or small sliver fresh orange peel

GLAZE

    2 tsps. cornstarch

    2 Tbsps. vinegar

    2 Tbsps. honey

TO PREPARE: 1. Clean the chicken and set aside liver and gizzards. Decide whether you are going to use PARBOILING INGREDIENTS A or PARBOILING INGREDIENTS B and prepare the items you will need as directed at left.

2. Bring 8–10 cups of water to boil in a *wok* or large pot. (There should be enough water to cover the chicken.) Add PARBOILING INGREDIENTS A or B and boil for 5 minutes. Carefully lower the chicken into the *wok* and boil for 10 minutes turning the bird occasionally. Remove the chicken from the *wok* and discard the water in which the chicken was boiled as well as the PARBOILING INGREDIENTS. Allow the chicken to cool a little, then pat it dry with a towel.

3. Make the GLAZE, first mixing the cornstarch with the vinegar and then adding the honey. Mix thoroughly. Smear the GLAZE evenly over the body of the chicken.

4. Devise an arrangement to hang the bird in a well-ventilated place. (Here's where ingenuity comes in. I have an S-shaped stainless-steel implement for this purpose, but you can also use some twine to tie the legs of the chicken together and hang the bird this way. And, if the weather is not helping to dry the bird, you can train a small fan on it to move things along.) Let the chicken dry. This will take 4–5 hours.

TO COOK: 1. When the chicken is thoroughly dry, heat 4–5 cups of cooking oil in a *wok* or deep fryer until very hot. Use enough oil so that the chicken will be at least half submerged when it is put in the *wok*. (See page 30 for directions on how to reclaim the cooking oil.) Carefully introduce the chicken and deep fry it, using a ladle to pour—ceaselessly and carefully—the heated oil over the top of the chicken. Turn the bird once. Continue deep frying over medium heat until it is a rich, deep brown color. Do not let the skin blacken. Remove and drain. Cool slightly.

2. Mix the SEASONINGS.

3. The traditional way of serving this dish is to cut the chicken into portion-sized pieces using a cleaver to cut through the

SEASONINGS
  1 Tbsp. salt
  2 tsps. ground Szechwan
    pepper
oil for deep frying

bones. Arrange the pieces on a platter as if they were a whole chicken. However, the chicken may look so good that you would prefer serving it uncut, carving it at table according to Western custom. Make little piles of the SEASONINGS on either end of the serving platter, or place the SEASONINGS in two small dishes to be passed at the table. Garnish with parsely and serve hot.

Ju-zi-pi Ji

橘子皮鷄

CHICKEN WITH FRESH ORANGE PEEL AND RED PEPPERS

I have occasionally seen this dish on the menu of some restaurants as Chen-pi Ji, *or "Chicken with Dried Orange Peel and Red Peppers," which it is not though the ingredients are similar. Emphasis is on the combination of the bitter taste of the charred fresh orange peel and the hotness of the red peppers.*

½ chicken breast, about ½ lb.
  when boned
the peel of one thin-skinned,
  Valencia-type orange
2 dried red peppers
MARINADE
  2 tsps. rice wine or dry
    sherry
  2 tsps. soy sauce
  1 tsp. salt
1 slice fresh ginger
4–6 green onions
SEASONINGS
  2 Tbsps. fresh orange juice
  1 Tbsp. sugar
  1 Tbsp. soy sauce
  1 tsp. vinegar
  1 tsp. sesame oil
4 Tbsps. oil

TO PREPARE: 1. Bone the chicken breast (see page 29) and cut the meat into bite-sized pieces. Mix the MARINADE, mix with chicken and marinate for 20 minutes.

2. Wash the orange thoroughly and dry it. Using a cleaver or sharp knife, cut off thin slices of peel about 1-inch by 1-inch (or slightly larger). Avoid cutting the pulp. Cut off the ends of the dried red peppers and shake out the seeds. Slice the ginger into slivers and cut the green onion into 1-inch lengths.

3. Squeeze 2 Tbsps. juice from the peeled orange into a small bowl and mix in the remaining SEASONINGS.

TO COOK: 1. Heat 4 Tbsps. cooking oil in a *wok* or large frying pan until very hot. Add orange peels and stir-fry over high heat until they start to char at the edges. Then add the dried red peppers. When they are black and the orange peels are deep brown, reduce the heat and remove both ingredients from the *wok* with a slotted spoon. (It is best to open the kitchen windows wide when stir-frying the red peppers.)

2. To the remaining oil, add the chicken pieces and cook over a medium fire until the chicken has turned white. Then add the ginger and green onion, and re-add the orange peels and red peppers. Finally add the SEASONINGS. Stir over medium or low heat for 2–3 minutes, or until the liquid has thickened and adheres to the chicken pieces. Check for salt and remove to a serving dish. Just before serving, sprinkle a few drops of sesame oil over the top. Serve hot.

Gui-fei Ji

貴 妃 鷄

YANG KUEI-FEI, OR EMPRESS, CHICKEN

Created in the 1920s in a Szechwanese restaurant in Shanghai, this dish took its name from Yang Kuei-fei, who was a celebrated imperial concubine in the T'ang dynasty (618–907). Reflecting the place of its origin, Gui-fei Ji probably has more in common with Shanghai cooking than with Szechwanese cuisine, but it is also a departure from both. Its rich sauce, made with port wine and sugar, is reminiscent of continental European food and suggests the influence of the International Settlement in Shanghai.

5–6 chicken wings
3–4 bamboo shoot tips, 6 to 7-
    inches long, or $\frac{1}{2}$ cup bam-
    boo shoot
2–3 green onions
2 large dried mushrooms
1 slice fresh ginger
$\frac{1}{2}$ tsp. sugar
SEASONINGS A
    2 cups chicken stock
    2 Tbsps. rice wine or dry
    sherry
    2 tsps. soy sauce
    1 tsp. salt
SEASONINGS B
    3 Tbsps. port wine*
    2 tsps. sugar
1 Tbsp. cornstarch mixed with
    2 Tbsps. water
approximately $\frac{1}{2}$ cup oil

*Or sustitute dry red wine and increase the sugar in SEASONINGS B by 1 tsp.

TO PREPARE: 1. Using the cleaver, cut each chicken wing in half at the joint. Wash thoroughly and pat dry.
2. Cut bamboo shoot tips into 3-inch lengths. Or, if you are using canned bamboo shoot, cut the slices into sticks. Cut the green onion into 4-inch lengths or, if they are thin and you do not want to include them in the final dish, tie each one end to end for easy retrieval later. Soak the dried mushrooms in warm water until softened, rinse well, cut off the tough stems, and cut the mushrooms into quarters.
3. Have the ingredients for SEASONINGS A and SEASONINGS B on hand. They do not have to be premixed and there is time to measure each ingredient as it is needed.

TO COOK: 1. Heat 4–5 Tbsps. of the cooking oil in a *wok* or large frying pan over a medium-high flame. Add the $\frac{1}{2}$ tsp. sugar, and stir it in the heated oil for a few moments and then add the chicken wings. Turn the heat to high if necessary and stir-fry the chicken wings quickly, ideally browning them slightly but not cooking them for over 1 minute. Remove and drain.
2. Add 4 Tbsps. of the cooking oil to the *wok* and heat over a medium-high flame. Add the green onion and bamboo shoot. Stir-fry for a few moments, then add the ginger slice, the chicken wings and the mushrooms. Stir-fry briefly, then add SEASONINGS A. Stir well and bring everything to a boil. Reduce the heat to very low and simmer for 15–20 minutes, or until the chicken wings are tender.
3. Remove and discard the ginger slice and the green onion (you can also try the dish with the green onion). Mix in SEASONINGS B, let simmer 30 seconds or so, then thicken the sauce by adding the cornstarch mixed with water (give it a quick stir first). Stir well. Remove to a serving platter and serve hot.

Xiang Su Ji-tui
香酥鷄腿

FRAGRANT CRISP–FRIED CHICKEN LEGS

Presteaming followed by breading and deep frying is a frequently used method to prepare whole poultry. Here chicken legs are called for but other cuts of chicken may be used with equally good results. The presteaming allows the chicken to absorb the salt and the flavors of the Szechwan pepper, green onion and ginger and makes it possible to deep fry the chicken pieces very quickly.

12 chicken drumsticks, or drumsticks and thighs
2–3 tsps. crushed or ground Szechwan pepper
5–6 tsps. salt
3–4 green onions or leeks
2 slices fresh ginger
1 Tbsp. rice wine or dry sherry
5 Tbsps. soy sauce
½ cup flour
oil for deep frying

TO PREPARE: 1. Wash chicken legs and pat them dry.
2. Heat a dry *wok* or small frying pan and add 1 heaping tsp. of the ground Szechwan pepper, heating until the pepper turns a deep brown color and the fragrance has become very strong. Add 3 tsps. of the salt and continue to heat for a few more seconds, mixing thoroughly. Remove to a bowl.
3. Carefully sprinkle the toasted Szechwan pepper and salt over each of the chicken legs. Arrange in a bowl and allow to stand for 2 hours.
4. Slice the green onion into 1-inch lengths, cut the ginger slices into 1-inch slivers. Arrange the chicken legs on a heatproof plate in a steamer (see page 22 for directions on how to improvise a steamer) and place the green onion pieces and ginger slivers over them. Then sprinkle 1 Tbsp. wine over the top. Cover and steam until the chicken is tender—about 40 minutes. Allow to cool.
5. Mix remaining Szechwan pepper and salt in a small bowl and set this mixture aside.

TO COOK: 1. When you are ready to deep fry the chicken legs, sprinkle each cooled drumstick with soy sauce, then roll each in the flour.
2. Heat several cups cooking oil in a *wok* or deep fryer and deep fry over medium-high heat, a few pieces at a time, until the chicken legs have turned a deep golden color. Drain each piece as you remove it from the *wok*. (See page 30 for directions on how to reclaim the cooking oil.) When all the chicken legs have been deep fried, arrange them on a large serving platter. The remaining salt and Szechwan pepper mixture is to be sprinkled over the chicken as one desires and should be placed in 1 or 2 piles on the side of the platter. Serve hot.

Jiang-bao Ya-kuai
FLASH–COOKED DUCK PIECES
COLOR: page 39

醬爆鴨塊

½ lb. duck meat, with bones
¼ cup bamboo shoot
1 green onion
4 slices fresh ginger
1 tsp. finely chopped garlic
1 Tbsp. sweet bean sauce or
    slightly more to taste
1 tsp. rice wine or dry sherry
2 Tbsps. chicken stock or water
½ tsp. sugar
1 tps. sesame oil
6 Tbsps. oil

TO PREPARE: 1. Clean the duck. Using a cleaver to cut through the bones, cut the meat into 1-inch pieces, bones and all.
2. Cut the bamboo shoot into bite-sized pieces. Cut the green onion into 1-inch lengths, slice the ginger into thin strips and chop the garlic finely.

TO COOK: 1. Heat 3 Tbsps. of the cooking oil in a *wok* or large frying pan over high heat. Add the duck and cook quickly until all the juices, though not the oil, have disappeared. Remove and drain.
2. Over a medium flame, heat 3 Tbsps. of the cooking oil in the *wok*, using any oil remaining from the previous step. Add the bamboo shoot and stir briefly. Then add the sweet bean sauce, wine, chopped garlic and ginger. Stir together until all ingredients are well heated and you can smell the garlic. Add the prefried duck pieces, green onion, sugar and stock. Turn the heat to low and stir until the liquid is considerably reduced and has thickened. Check for salt. Remove to a serving dish, dribble the sesame oil over the top and serve hot.

Zi-jiang Ya-kuai
DUCK WITH FRESH GINGER AND GREEN PEPPER

子薑鴨塊

¾ lb. boned duck breast, or leg
    meat
2–3 Tbsps. fresh ginger (as young
    and juicy as possible)
½–1 green pepper
2 fresh or dried red peppers
1 green onion
SEASONINGS
    2 Tbsps. rice wine or sherry
    1 tsp. finely chopped garlic
    2 tsps. sweet bean sauce
    1 Tbsp. hot bean sauce
    2 tsps. soy sauce

TO PREPARE: 1. Clean the duck and cut the meat into 1-inch pieces.
2. Cut the ginger into thin slices. Cut off the top and seed the green pepper and cut it into 1-inch pieces. Cut off the top and seed the red peppers and cut into small shreds. If you are using dried red peppers, soak them in warm water until softened and then seed and cut them into small shreds. Cut the green onion into ¾ or 1-inch sections. Chop the garlic finely.
3. Mix the SEASONINGS in a cup or small bowl.

TO COOK: 1. Heat 4–6 Tbsps. of the cooking oil in a *wok* or large frying pan until very hot. Add the duck pieces and fry, stirring, over heat until the liquid but not the oil has cooked

1 cup chicken stock
1 tsp. sugar
1 Tbsp. red oil (optional) or
  sesame oil
approximately ½ cup oil

away. This will take several minutes. Remove with a slotted spoon and drain.

2. To the oil remaining in the *wok*, add a few more table-spoons of the cooking oil so that the oil in the *wok* is equal to 4–6 Tbsps. Over a high flame, heat the oil and then add the ginger and red pepper shreds and fry for 5–10 seconds. Add the prefried duck pieces, the green pepper and SEASON-INGS. Stir once. Add the chicken stock, stir, and reduce the heat. Simmer for 4–5 minutes, then turn the heat as high as possible. Add sugar, green onion and red oil. Stir well. Check for salt, remove to a serving dish and serve hot.

Feng-gan Cao-gu   鳳肝草菇
CHICKEN LIVERS WITH STRAW MUSHROOMS

8 chicken livers
1 can straw mushrooms, or ½
  lb. small fresh mushrooms,
  washed and stemmed
PREFRYING INGREDIENTS
    2 tsps. rice wine or dry
    sherry
    2 slices ginger
    1 green onion
    1 tsp. salt
    4 Tbsps. soy sauce
    1 tsp. sugar
    3 pieces star anise
    1 cup water
1 tsp. cornstarch mixed with 2
  tsps. water
2 tsps. sesame oil
approximately ⅔ cup oil

TO PREPARE: 1. Clean the chicken livers and cut away any tough parts. Leave them whole or cut them into halves or thirds. Place in a *wok* or small saucepan and add the PREFRYING INGREDIENTS. Bring to a boil and simmer for 20 minutes, stirring once or twice. Remove livers and drain, discarding the stock. Rinse and drain the straw mushrooms.

2. Heat 4 Tbsps. of the cooking oil in a *wok* or large frying pan until hot. Add the chicken livers and fry over medium heat for about 2 minutes. Remove together with juices and oil.

TO COOK: Heat about 5 Tbsps. of the cooking oil in the *wok* until hot. Add mushrooms. Fry quickly over high heat until the mushrooms are heated through. Reduce the heat and add the fried liver along with the liquids retained in Step 2, above. Cook for 2 minutes, then stir the cornstarch mixed with 2 tsps. water and add to the *wok*. Stir. When the sauce has thickened slightly, check for salt. Sprinkle sesame oil over the top, remove to a serving dish and serve hot.

Yu-xiang Si-jian

魚香四件

CHICKEN GIBLETS WITH YU–XIANG SAUCE

This version of Yu-xiang sauce is milder than those included in the recipes for Eggplant with Yu-xiang Sauce (see page 93) and Pork Liver with Yu-xiang Sauce (see page 75). Since the flavor of chicken giblets or liver is comparatively delicate, the amounts of ginger and, especially, of garlic are reduced in this recipe. Fresh red peppers, or dried red peppers if fresh ones are unavailable, replace the more strongly flavored hot bean sauce.

½ lb. chicken giblets, or only chicken livers

MARINADE

 2 tsps. cornstarch

 2 tsps. rice wine or dry sherry

 ½ tsp. salt

2–4 fresh or dried red peppers

1–2 dried mushrooms (optional)

5–8 slices bamboo shoot (optional, or substitute this for the dried mushroom)

1 Tbsp. finely chopped green onion

1 tsp. finely chopped fresh ginger

1 tsp. finely chopped garlic

SEASONINGS

 2 tsps. cornstarch

 2 tsps. soy sauce

 2 tsps. vinegar

 1 tsp. red oil

 1 tsp. sugar

 ½ tsp. salt

 ½ tsp. black pepper

 ¼ tsp. ground Szechwan pepper

5–7 Tbsps. oil

TO PREPARE: 1. Clean giblets, cut away any part you will not want to eat (a purely subjective matter) and cut them into thin slices, about ¼-inch thick or so. Make the MARINADE, mix with the giblets and marinate at least 10–15 minutes. 2. Slice the red peppers in half lengthwise, remove seeds with the tip of a knife and cut the peppers into flakes. If you are using dried red peppers, soak them in warm water until softened and then proceed to seed and cut them into flakes. If you are using dried mushrooms, soak them in warm water until softened, rinse well, cut away tough stems, and slice into bite-sized pieces. If you are using bamboo shoot, slice into bite-sized pieces. Chop the green onion, ginger and garlic finely.

3. In a bowl, mix the SEASONINGS, first mixing the cornstarch with the soy sauce and vinegar and then adding the other ingredients.

TO COOK: 1. Heat 3–4 Tbsps. of the cooking oil in a *wok* or large frying pan until fairly hot. Drain any excess marinade and add the giblets, tossing them over high heat until they loose their pink color and turn grey. Do not overcook or the giblets will be dry and tough. Remove and drain.

2. Heat another 2–3 Tbsps. of the cooking oil in the *wok*. Add the mushrooms and/or bamboo shoot and the red pepper flakes. Toss for 15–20 seconds, or until you can smell the red peppers. Then add the prefried chicken giblets, green onion, ginger and garlic. Toss for a few seconds until the giblets are thoroughly reheated, then stir the SEASONINGS and add to the *wok*. Stir over heat until the sauce thickens and adheres to the meat. Remove to a serving dish and serve hot.

BEEF AND LAMB

Beef and lamb are eaten much less in China than other meats. The consumption of lamb in particular seems to have been largely limited to a few northern provinces. Beef in China is usually water buffalo or ox, especially in the south. These meats tend to be somewhat tough and have a heavier taste than cattle beef. For most purposes, the most inexpensive cuts are the best substitutes and are the easiest to use.

Yu-xiang Yang-gan
LAMB LIVER WITH YU–XIANG SAUCE

魚香羊肝

1¼–1½ lb. lamb liver
MARINADE
    1 Tbsp. cornstarch
    1 Tbsp. rice wine or dry sherry
    2 Tbsps. soy sauce
    1–2 tsps. salt
2–3 Tbsps. finely chopped green onion
1–2 Tbsps. finely chopped fresh ginger
1–2 Tbsps. finely chopped garlic
1–2 Tbsps. hot bean sauce
2 tsps. salt
4–5 pieces wood ear
SEASONINGS
    2 Tbsps. cornstarch
    2 Tbsps. soy sauce
    1–2 tsps. sugar
    2 tsps. vinegar
    1 Tbsp. sesame oil
¼ cup oil

TO PREPARE: 1. Cut away any tough portions of the liver, and slice thinly into about ¼-inch widths. Make the MARINADE first mixing the cornstarch with the wine and soy sauce and then add the salt. Mix with the meat and marinate at least 10–15 minutes.

2. Chop the green onion, ginger and garlic finely. Soak the wood ear in warm water until softened, rinse well, cut away tough parts and shred it.

3. Mix the SEASONINGS in a cup or small bowl, first mixing the cornstarch with the soy sauce and vinegar and adding the sesame oil.

TO COOK: 1. Heat ¼ cup cooking oil in a *wok* or large frying pan until very hot. Drain any excess MARINADE from the meat, add the liver slices and cook quickly until the meat is grey.

2. Immediately add the green onion, ginger, garlic, hot bean sauce, salt and wood ear. When the hot bean sauce is well mixed with the other ingredients and they have taken on its reddish color, add the SEASONINGS (stir once before adding to the *wok*). Give everything a good stir. Check for salt. Remove to a serving dish and serve hot.

59

Cong-bao Yang-rou

FLASH–FRIED LAMB WITH GREEN ONION

葱爆羊肉

COLOR: page 40

This recipe is from Shantung Province in North China. The lamb should be sliced very thinly and cooked very quickly.

¾ lb. leg of lamb, or another
   lamb cut

MARINADE
    2 Tbsps. cooking oil
    2 Tbsps. rice wine or dry
    sherry
    2 Tbsps. soy sauce
    ½ tsp. salt
    ½ tsp. ground Szechwan
    pepper
3–4 green onions, or 2 leeks
3–4 small cloves garlic

SEASONINGS
    2 Tbsps. soy sauce
    1 Tbsp. vinegar
    1 Tbsp. sesame oil
½ cup peanut oil*

TO PREPARE: 1. To facilitate the cutting of the meat, freeze the lamb first and slice it as thinly as possible, into ⅛-inch widths or less. Make the MARINADE, first heating the 2 Tbsps. cooking oil in the *wok* until hot. Transfer the heated oil to a small bowl and add the other MARINADE ingredients. Mix with the lamb slices and marinate at least 15 minutes.
2. Cut the green onion or leeks into 3-inch sections and then lengthwise into shreds. Cut the garlic into thin slices.
3. Mix the SEASONINGS in a cup or small bowl.

TO COOK: 1. Heat ½ cup peanut oil (or other vegetable oil) in a *wok* or large frying pan until very hot. Add the garlic slices and stir-fry for a few seconds. Pour the excess MARINADE off the lamb and then add the lamb slices to the oil. The lamb slices are cooked as soon as they turn white. (It is extremely important to cook the lamb very quickly, almost instantaneously. So unless you have a stove that can keep the oil very, very hot, it may be better to cook the lamb a few slices at a time, removing and draining each batch as it cooks. When all the lamb slices have been cooked, replace the previously cooked portions in the *wok*.)
2. When all the lamb is white in color, add the green onion or leek shreds. Keep the flame on high. Add the SEASONINGS. Give all ingredients a good stir. Remove to a serving dish and serve hot.

* Peanut oil is preferred in making this dish because this type of oil retains its high temperature in cooking better than other vegetable oils.

Gan-bian Niu-rou-si

乾煸牛肉絲

DRY–FRIED BEEF WITH CARROTS AND CELERY
COLOR: page 35

1 lb. beef, any cut, sirloin steak is the best

$\frac{1}{3}$–$\frac{1}{2}$ lb. celery

1–2 carrots, depending on size*

3 fresh or dried red peppers

1 green onion

1 tsp. finely chopped ginger

2 tsps. finely chopped garlic

1–1$\frac{1}{2}$ Tbsps. hot bean sauce (optional)

2 tsps. sweet bean sauce

1 Tbsp. rice wine or dry sherry

1$\frac{1}{2}$ tsp. salt

1 tsp. sugar

$\frac{1}{2}$ tsp. ground Szechwan pepper

2 tsps. sesame oil

1-tsp. 2 Tbsps. red oil (optional)

9 Tbsps. oil or lard

*If this ingredient is omitted, increase the amount of celery used and add $\frac{1}{2}$ tsp. sugar

TO PREPARE: 1. Cut the meat into very thin slices, about $\frac{1}{8}$-inch thick, and then into very narrow shreds, about $\frac{1}{8}$-inch wide. Cutting is easier if the meat is frozen.

2. Remove the leaves and base of the celery, wash the celery thoroughly and cut it into 1-inch pieces. Peel the carrots and cut them into fine shreds, about 2$\frac{1}{2}$–3-inches long. Top and seed the red peppers and cut them lengthwise into fine shreds. If using dried red peppers, soak them in warm water until softened and then seed and cut them into fine shreds. Cut the green onion into $\frac{1}{2}$-inch lengths or smaller.

3. Chop the ginger and the garlic as finely as possible. Have the other ingredients at hand.

TO COOK: 1. Heat 3 Tbsps. of the cooking oil or lard in a *wok* or large frying pan until very hot. Add the celery and carrots and $\frac{1}{2}$ tsp. of the salt. Toss over high heat briefly until the vegetables are partially cooked. Remove and drain.

2. Heat 6 Tbsps. of the cooking oil or lard in the *wok* until very hot, then allow to cool slightly. Add the beef shreds and cook over a medium fire, stirring constantly. (If the juices stick to the sides of the *wok*, they will soon char and ruin the flavor of the beef. If this begins to happen, immediately remove the beef, discard the oil, clean the *wok* and start over with another 6 Tbsps. cooking oil or lard.) Cook the beef evenly and thoroughly and, using chopsticks or another utensil, keep the beef shreds from sticking together while cooking. Cook, tossing frequently, until the beef has turned a dark color and has become dry looking and stiff—about 10 minutes.

3. When the beef is thoroughly cooked, add the hot bean sauce and the sweet bean sauce, red peppers, garlic, about half the green onion, the remaining salt and the rice wine. Stir well. When the smell of the garlic and bean sauces is noticeable, add the prefried celery and carrots. Continue to stir until the celery and carrots are reheated, then at the last minute add the sugar, ginger, remaining green onion, Szechwan pepper and sesame oil. Stir for 20–30 seconds. Taste and check for saltiness and hotness and add more salt or the red oil if you desire. Remove to a serving dish and serve hot.

Hong-shau Niu-rou

BRAISED BEEF

紅燒牛肉

1 lb. boneless stewing beef
2 green onions
2 slices fresh ginger
4 cups pork or chicken stock
3 pieces star anise
5 Tbsps. soy sauce
3 Tbsps. rice wine or dry sherry
1 tsp. sugar
5 Tbsps. oil or lard

OPTIONAL
5–6 Szechwan peppercorns
$\frac{1}{4}$ cup bamboo shoot
2 Tbsps. brown bean sauce, or
   1 Tbsp. hot bean sauce

TO PREPARE: 1. In a *wok* or pot, bring to boil enough water to cover the beef. Add the entire piece of beef and simmer it over low heat for about 20 minutes. Remove and drain. When cooled, cut the beef into bite-sized chunks about 1-inch thick.
2. Cut the green onion into 2-inch lengths.

TO COOK: 1. Heat 5 Tbsps. cooking oil or lard in a *wok* or large frying pan until very hot. Add the green onion lengths and the ginger slices and stir until the onion-and-ginger smell is strong. Immediately add the stock, star anise, soy sauce, wine and parboiled beef squares. Bring to a boil and simmer briefly over medium heat.
2. Reduce the flame and simmer over low heat until the meat is very tender and the stock is heavy. Add the sugar, stir once, check for salt. Remove to a serving bowl and serve hot.

NOTE: For Szechwan-style Braised Beef, follow these additional steps:
a.) Add the Szechwan peppercorns along with the stock, soy sauce, etc. (TO COOK: Step 1, above)
b.) Cut the bamboo shoot into bite-sized pieces, about 1-inch square and $\frac{1}{2}$-inch thick. In a small pot, bring one cup of water to boil. Add the bamboo shoot and parboil for a few minutes. Remove and rinse thoroughly with cold water. Add the bamboo shoot to the beef and stock partway through the simmering process. (TO COOK: Step 2, above)
c.) In a separate *wok* or small frying pan, heat 2 Tbsps. cooking oil, add the brown bean paste or hot bean paste and stir-fry for several seconds. Add this ingredient to the beef in the last minutes of simmering and before the addition of the sugar. (TO COOK: Step 2, above.)

Yu-xiang Niu-rou-si

魚香牛肉絲

BEEF SHREDS WITH YU–XIANG SAUCE

The yu-xiang sauce in this dish is made with red oil and fresh or dried red peppers rather than with hot bean sauce.

½ lb. beef, any cut

MARINADE

    1 tsp. cornstarch mixed with 2 tsps. water

    ½ tsp. salt

    1 egg white

¼ cup bamboo shoot*

2 fresh or dried red peppers

SEASONINGS

    3 tsps. finely chopped green onion

    2 tsps. finely chopped garlic

    2 tsps. finely chopped fresh ginger

    1 tsp. cornstarch mixed with 2 tsps. water

    1 tsp. rice wine or dry sherry

    2 tsps. soy sauce

    1 tsp. vinegar

    1 tsp. red oil or sesame oil

    ½ tsp. ground Szechwan pepper

    1 tsp. sugar

approximately ½ cup oil

*Or substitute an equal volume of wood ear or finely shredded carrot. If using the wood ear, soak in warm water until softened, rinse well and cut away any tough parts.

TO PREPARE: 1. Cut the meat into very thin slices, about ⅛-inch thick, and then into very narrow shreds, about ⅛-inch wide. Make the MARINADE, first mixing the cornstarch with the water and then adding the salt and egg white. Stir thoroughly. Mix the MARINADE with the meat and marinate for 10 minutes.

2. Cut the bamboo shoot into very thin shreds about 1½-inches long. Top and seed the fresh red peppers and cut them into very thin shreds. If using dried red peppers, soak them in warm water until softened and then proceed to seed and cut them into shreds. Chop the green onion, garlic and ginger finely.

3. Mix the SEASONINGS in a small bowl, first mixing the cornstarch with the wine and soy sauce, then adding the remaining ingredients.

TO COOK: 1. Heat 4–6 Tbsps. of the cooking oil in a *wok* or large frying pan until very hot. Pour the excess MARINADE off the beef and add the beef shreds to the oil. Stir-fry for about 30 seconds and then remove with a slotted spoon and drain.

2. Add enough cooking oil to what remains in the *wok* to equal 4–6 Tbsps. Heat until very hot. Add the bamboo shoot (or wood ear or carrots) and red pepper shreds and stir-fry briefly. Add the prefried beef shreds. Cook for 10 seconds or so, drain off any excess oil, then add the SEASONINGS (stir once before adding to the *wok*). Stir over a medium heat until everything is mixed and heated. Remove to a serving dish and serve hot.

PORK

Pork is undoubtedly the most widely consumed meat in China, as well as in the rest of East Asia. Chinese pork is stronger in flavor and is more of a red-meat than American pork. In China, the method of butchering the animal differs completely from Western methods—the meat is almost always cut with the grain, not across it, and most cuts are boneless.

With a few exceptions, pork is always fried. Since it is usually cut into thin slices or shreds, it is possible to cook it throughly without the meat becoming dry and overdone. In most cases, pork is cooked with spices and sauces, and then combined with fried vegetables. In western and northern Chinese cooking, the sauces that are most commonly used are hot bean sauce (*la-dou-ban jiang*) or sweet bean sauce (*tian-mian jiang*) or a combination of the two. Ginger is frequently used with pork, garlic occasionally.

When buying pork, an inexpensive roast is the most practical choice. Pork chops may seem less expensive at the grocery store, but there will be considerable waste when you cut the meat from the bone, and it is difficult to cut the boned fillet into smaller pieces unless it is frozen. (If you use pork chops anyway, as I sometimes do, use the bones for stock.)

Mu-xu Rou
PORK WITH EGG AND WOOD EAR

木 須 肉

The character 須, *pronounced "xu" and used above, was originally* 樨. *Written in this way* (木樨), *the compound means "cassia," or "Chinese cinnamon," and the dish took this name because the eggs are said to resemble the yellow blossoms of this shrub. A dish from northern China,* Mu-xu Rou *has recently become popular in the United States. Mild.*

½ lb. lean pork
MARINADE
    2 tsps. cornstarch
    2 tsps. soy sauce
    2 tsps. rice wine or dry sherry
    ½ tsp. salt

To PREPARE: 1. Slice pork thinly, then cut into shreds about 1½-inches long and ¼-inch wide. Make MARINADE by mixing cornstarch with soy sauce and wine and adding salt. Mix with pork and marinate at least 15 minutes.

2. Soak wood ear in warm water until softened, rinse well, cut away tough parts and cut into shreds. Shred the bamboo shoot and green onion. Chop the ginger finely.

5–6 pieces wood ear
5–6 slices bamboo shoot
1 green onion
1 Tbsp. finely chopped ginger
3 eggs
½ tsp. salt
1 tsp. soy sauce
SEASONINGS
    1 Tbsp. rice wine or dry
    sherry
    1 Tbsp. soy sauce
    ¼ cup pork or chicken
    stock or water
    ½ tsp. salt
    2 tsps. sesame oil
approximately ⅔ cup oil

3. Beat eggs together, adding ½ tsp. salt and 1 tsp. soy sauce.
4. Mix SEASONINGS in a cup or small bowl.

To COOK: 1. Heat 4 Tbsps. cooking oil in a *wok* or large frying pan and add eggs, stirring over a medium flame. As eggs coalesce, break them up so that the result is many small pieces of dry scrambled egg. Remove from *wok*.

2. Heat 4–6 Tbsps. cooking oil in the *wok* over a high flame. Drain any excess MARINADE and add pork shreds, tossing the meat until it turns white. Add the green onion and ginger. Toss briefly. Then add bamboo shoot and wood ear. Toss together for a few seconds. Add SEASONINGS and scrambled egg pieces. Mix over flame until everything is well heated. Remove to a serving dish and serve hot.

Jiang-bao Rou   醬爆肉
FLASH–COOKED PORK WITH PEKING SAUCE

Not at all hot, this dish is a bit spicy with the heavy, sweet flavor that sweet bean sauce gives.

½ lb. lean pork
MARINADE
    1 Tbsp. cornstarch mixed
    with 2 Tbsps. water
    ½ tsp. salt
    1 egg white
2 tsps. finely chopped fresh ginger
2 tsps. finely chopped green onion
3 two-inch sections of green onion
1 Tbsp. sweet bean sauce
SEASONINGS
    2 tsps. rice wine or dry
    sherry
    1 tsp. sugar
    2 tsps. soy sauce
    ½ tsp. salt
approximately ¾ cup oil

To PREPARE: 1. Slice pork thinly, then cut into shreds, about 1 to 1½-inches long and ¼-inch wide. Make MARINADE by mixing cornstarch with 2 Tbsps. water, add salt, beat in egg white and mix with pork. Marinate about 15 minutes.

2. Chop ginger and green onion finely. Chop the 2-inch sections of green onion lengthwise into thin shreds.

3. Mix the SEASONINGS in a cup or small bowl.

To COOK: 1. Heat ½ cup cooking oil in a *wok* or large frying pan over high heat. Pour off and discard excess MARINADE from the pork. Add the pork shreds and cook very fast, for 10–12 seconds. The pork shreds should all turn white. (If the heat source is insufficient to cook all the pork in 10–12 seconds, it is better to cook just a few shreds at a time.) Remove pork and drain.

2. Add about ¼ cup cooking oil to the *wok* and heat. Add ginger, chopped green onion and sweet bean sauce. Cook over medium heat for about 1 minute. Then increase heat, adding pork shreds and SEASONINGS. Cook for another 30 seconds or so, stirring thoroughly, then remove to serving plate. Arrange the green onion shreds over the top and serve hot.

Shi-zi Tou

"LIONS' HEADS"—SZECHWAN-STYLE MEATBALLS

COLOR: page 37

This dish is particularly good in winter, something to have as a part of a large dinner with many other things. It makes four very large meatballs—they're very filling and half of one is all I ever want to eat at one time.

1½ lbs. "mixed meat," equal proportions of fairly fatty pork and beef, chopped or ground together

2 Tbsps. finely chopped garlic

2 Tbsps. finely chopped fresh ginger

1–2 green onions

4 Tbsps. soy sauce

1 Tbsp. cornstarch

2½ tsps. salt

approximately 1 lb. greens (any tasty greens will do—even brussel sprouts are good)

COATING

    4–5 Tbsps. cornstarch

    ½ cup soy sauce

4 Tbsps. sesame oil

approximately ¾ cup oil

SEASONINGS

    4 Tbsps. rice wine or dry sherry

    2 Tbsps. soy sauce

    1 Tbsp. sugar

2 Tbsps. cornstarch mixed with 4 Tbsps. water.

TO PREPARE: 1. If you bought unground meat, start by chopping the pork and beef finely and mixing them together. Do not discard fatty pieces—chop them also and mix with the rest of the meat. If you are using commercially ground meat, chop it up some more to break up the larger pieces and then mix the pork and beef thoroughly.

2. Chop the garlic, ginger and green onion finely. In a cup or small bowl, mix 4 Tbsps. soy sauce with 1 Tbsp. cornstarch and 2 tsps. of the salt.

3. Thoroughly mix the chopped meat, garlic, ginger, green onion and soy-sauce-cornstarch-salt mixture together. Divide the meat into equal parts and form into 4 large meatballs.

4. Prepare the COATING. In a medium-sized bowl, mix the cornstarch and soy sauce together to make a thin paste. Pour the 4 Tbsps. sesame oil onto a large plate. Roll each meatball in the bowl with the COATING until covered, then remove to the plate which holds the sesame oil. (If the COATING seems to be too thin, add more cornstarch. If necessary make more COATING.) When all four meatballs have been coated and then rolled in sesame oil, dribble a little more sesame oil over each.

5. Cut greens into bite-sized pieces.

TO COOK: 1. Heat about ¼ cup of the cooking oil in *wok* or large frying pan, add the greens or your choice of vegetable, plus the remaining ½ tsp. salt. Toss quickly for 10–15 seconds, then remove and drain. Keep the greens warm.

2. Heat about ½ cup cooking oil in the *wok* until fairly hot and, using a spatula or large spoon and handling the meatballs carefully to avoid breaking them, add them one at a time. Fry in the hot oil, turning occasionally until each meatball is lightly browned on all sides. Add more oil if necessary.

3. Remove meatballs from the *wok* and drain excess oil from the *wok*. Put the meatballs back into the *wok* or frying pan and add almost enough water to cover them. Add SEASONINGS. Bring to a boil and simmer over a medium fire for about 35 minutes, turning the meatballs over once about halfway through. (Do not allow water to simmer away.)

2. To serve, remove the meatballs to a raised-edge serving

platter and arrange the previously fried greens around them. Use the juice remaining in the *wok* for gravy. Check the liquid for salt, adding more salt or soy sauce if necessary. Keeping the *wok* or frying pan over a medium flame, add the 2 Tbsps. cornstarch mixed with 4 Tbsps. water or enough cornstarch-and-water to thicken the remaining juices to the consistency of medium-heavy gravy. Pour over the meatballs and greens and serve hot.

Yu-xiang Rou-si
魚香肉絲

SHREDDED PORK WITH YU-XIANG SAUCE

Yu-xiang sauce includes garlic, ginger, hot bean sauce and green onion and is one of the eight basic methods of Szechwanese cooking. Expect something hot and spicy, maybe slightly sweet and sour. With some variation, this basic method can be applied to many different kinds of foods. Though yu-xiang sauce is most frequently used with eggplant, liver and kidneys, this recipe uses pork. You can also substitute beef (see page 63).

$\frac{1}{2}$ lb. lean pork
MARINADE
    2 tsps. cornstarch
    2 tsps. soy sauce
    $\frac{1}{2}$ tsp. salt
2–3 tsps. finely chopped garlic
2 tsps. finely chopped fresh ginger
1–2 Tbsps. finely chopped green onion
1 Tbsps. finely chopped water chestnuts (optional)
10 pieces wood ear
1 Tbsp. hot bean sauce, or 3–4 seeded and finely chopped dried red peppers
SEASONINGS
    2 tsps. cornstarch
    2 tsps. rice wine or dry sherry
    1 Tbsp. soy sauce
    1–1$\frac{1}{2}$ tsps. sugar
    $\frac{1}{2}$–1 tsp. salt
    1–2 tsps. sesame oil
approximately $\frac{1}{3}$ cup oil

TO PREPARE: 1. Slice pork thinly, then cut into shreds about 1 to 1$\frac{1}{2}$-inches long and $\frac{1}{2}$-inch wide. Make MARINADE and mix with pork shreds and marinate at least 10–15 minutes.
2. Chop garlic, ginger, green onion and water chestnuts finely. Soak wood ear in warm water until softened, rinse well, cut away tough parts and cut into shreds.
3. In a cup or small bowl, mix the SEASONINGS, first mixing the cornstarch with the wine and soy sauce before adding the other ingredients.

TO COOK: 1. In a *wok* or large frying pan, heat 4–5 Tbsps. cooking oil until very hot. Drain any excess MARINADE and add the pork shreds and toss until the shreds turn white. Then drain and immediately remove to a side dish or a serving bowl. Save the remaining cooking oil for the next step.
2. Add 1–2 Tbsps. of the cooking oil to that in the *wok*. Heat until very hot and add garlic, ginger, green onion and hot bean sauce. When the red color of the hot bean sauce begins to be absorbed throughout the dish, add the wood ear, water chestnuts and the prefried pork shreds. Toss until the pork shreds are thoroughly reheated. Then give the SEASONINGS a stir and add them to the *wok*. Continue to stir over medium heat until the sauce starts to thicken and the food begins to adhere to itself. Remove to serving plate and serve hot.

Hui-guo Rou

TWICE–COOKED PORK

COLOR: page 37

回 鍋 肉

Another dish which has become very well known outside China, Hui-guo Rou literally means "returned-to-the-pot pork" for the pork is first boiled in one large piece, then cooled, sliced, and finally fried with other ingredients. The recipe below calls for 1/2 pound pork loin or rump. However, the most practical way to prepare this dish is to buy a small roast (enough to prepare this dish several times) and to boil the entire piece. Cut off what you need and then refrigerate or freeze the rest. The remaining pork can be used to make Twice-cooked Pork again or in other recipes such as Cold White Pork with Garlic (see page 70).

½ lb. pork, loin or rump

STOCK

    1 green onion, cut into 3-inch lengths

    1 slice fresh ginger

1–3 green peppers, depending on size

½ tsp. salt

3 pieces yellow, dry *dou-fu* (optional)*

1 tsp. finely chopped fresh ginger (optional)

1–2 tsps. coarsely chopped garlic

1–2 green onions

½–1 Tbsp. hot bean sauce

4½ tsps. sweet bean sauce

SEASONINGS

    1 tsp. wine or sherry

    1 Tbsp. soy sauce

    1 tsp. sugar

    ½–1 tsp. salt

approximately ¾ cup oil

* This ingredient is pretty difficult to find even at Chinese grocery stores. Keep trying.

TO PREPARE: 1. Bring enough water to cover the pork to boil in a *wok* or pot. Add the STOCK ingredients and let boil for a few minutes. Add the pork and gently boil until the pork is tender. Test with a fork. Depending on the size of the pork roast, it will take from 20–30 minutes. Remove and allow to cool. Strain and use the broth for pork stock in other recipes, if desired.

2. Cut the pork into very thin slices, about the size of potato chips. The fatty parts are considered a delicacy and should not be removed.

3. Top and seed the green pepper and cut into bite-sized sections, about 1-inch pieces. Slice the yellow, dry *dou-fu* thinly. Chop the ginger finely and the garlic coarsely. Cut the green onion into 1½-inch lengths.

4. Mix the SEASONINGS in a cup or small bowl.

TO COOK: 1. Heat ¾ cup cooking oil until very hot in a *wok* or large frying pan. Add green pepper and sprinkle with ½ tsp. salt. Toss quickly for 5–15 seconds until the peppers are covered with oil and heated. Remove and drain. Reheat any remaining oil (it may be necessary to add 3–4 Tbsps. more oil) until very hot. Add yellow, dry *dou-fu* and toss until pieces are heated. Remove and drain.

2. Heat only 4–6 Tbsps. cooking oil left from the previous step in the *wok*. Add the slices of boiled pork roast. Toss for 10–15 seconds. If there seems to be too much oil, pour some off. Then add the hot bean sauce, sweet bean sauce, garlic and ginger. Toss until the pork is coated with the sauces and everything is heated. Then add the green onion lengths, green pepper, yellow dry *dou-fu* and SEASONINGS. Stir over heat until everything is well mixed and smells good. Check for salt, remove to a serving dish and serve hot.

Shui-hu Rou

"WATER MARGIN" PORK

水滸肉

The Water Margin (Shui-hu chuan) *is one of the most famous of all traditional Chinese novels. Written during the Ming dynasty (1368–1644), it records the adventures of a band of errant heroes in northern China during the disordered times of the twelfth century. This spicy dish takes its name from the exotic fare of Mr. Jang's wineshop described in the book's twenty-sixth chapter.*

½ lb. lean pork
MARINADE
    2 tsps. cornstarch mixed
    with 4 tsps. water
    ½ egg white
¼ lb. bean sprouts
½ tsp. salt
2–3 dried red peppers
9–10 Szechwan peppercorns
2–4 garlic cloves
SEASONINGS
    1 cup pork or chicken stock
    1 tsp. salt
    ½ tsp. sugar
    ½ tsp. black pepper
    2 tsps. soy sauce
approximately ⅔ cup oil

TO PREPARE: 1. Slice pork thinly, then cut into strips about 2 to 3-inches long and ½ to ¾-inches wide. If desired, remove the dark ends from the bean sprouts; otherwise simply wash and drain them and use whole. Remove ends and seeds from dried red peppers. Cut the garlic into thin slices and then into slivers.

2. Moisten the pork with a few tsps. water. To make the MARINADE, mix the cornstarch with 4 tsps. water and beat in the egg white. Mix with the pork.

3. Mix the SEASONINGS in a small bowl.

TO COOK: 1. Heat 4–6 Tbsps. cooking oil in a *wok* or large frying pan over high heat. When the oil is very hot, add the bean sprouts and ½ tsp. salt. Stir-fry quickly until the bean sprouts are well heated. Remove to a serving dish.

2. Heat an additional 4–6 Tbsps. cooking oil over high heat. Add the dried red peppers, stir briefly, then add the Szechwan peppercorns. Stir once or twice and then immediately reduce heat and remove the cooked peppers and peppercorns with a slotted spoon (removing the peppercorns can be difficult). On a chopping board, cut the red peppers into slivers or fine pieces. Crush the peppercorns with the side of a cleaver and then chop them a few times. Put both ingredients aside.

3. Reheat the oil remaining in the *wok* over a high fire. When the oil is hot, add the SEASONINGS (be careful—it will splatter a little) and cook briefly. Then, just before the liquid has boiled down, add the pork slices (drain any excess MARINADE) and garlic slivers. Reduce heat slightly and stir-fry until just after the pork has turned white and seems done. Reduce heat and remove the meat from the *wok*, arranging it on the bed of fried bean sprouts in the serving dish. Sprinkle the chopped red reppers and Szechwan peppercorns over the meat, then pour the liquid remaining in the *wok* over the top. If you like a little juicier dish, try heating an additional 2–4 Tbsps. cooking oil in the *wok* and pouring this over the pork and beans sprouts too. Serve hot.

Suan-ni Bai-rou
COLD WHITE PORK WITH GARLIC

蒜泥白肉

This is an easy-to-prepare dish and good for entertaining because everything can be done ahead of time. It is also a quick way of using precooked meat left from making such recipes as Twice-cooked Pork (see page 68).

1 lb. pork, loin or rump is excellent but other cuts are good too
1 green onion
2 large slices fresh ginger
1 tsp. salt
SEASONINGS
    5 tsps. soy sauce
    1/2 tsp. salt
    1 tsp. vinegar
    2 tsps. sesame oil (optional)
    2 Tbsps. red oil
    1 1/2 Tbsps. crushed or very finely chopped garlic
    1 Tbsp. water
    1 tsp. sugar

TO PREPARE AND COOK: 1. Cut the green onion in long lengths and cut two large slices of fresh ginger.
2. Place the whole piece of pork in a *wok* or large pot, add water to cover the meat and add the green onion, ginger and salt. Bring to a boil and cook over a medium flame for 20–30 minutes or until the pork is tender. Remove pork. When cool, cut the meat into very thin slices. Arrange the slices on a serving platter. Strain and use the broth for pork stock in other recipes, if desired.

TO ASSEMBLE: Mix the SEASONINGS in a cup or small bowl. Let stand for 10–15 minutes. To serve, simply pour SEASONINGS over the cold pork. Garnish with parsley.

Cong-bao Rou-pian
FLASH–FRIED PORK SLICES AND GREEN ONION

葱爆肉片

Not at all hot, this dish is actually Shantung cooking. The same basic recipe can be used with other meats such as beef.

1/2 lb. lean pork
MARINADE
    1 Tbsp. rice wine or dry sherry
    1 Tbsp. soy sauce
    1/2 tsp. salt
    1/2 tsp. ground Szechwan pepper, or black pepper
    2 Tbsps. oil
3–4 green onions
2 tsps. chopped garlic

TO PREPARE: 1. Slice pork thinly, into 1/8-inch wide slices or thinner if possible, then cut into shreds, about 1/2 to 1-inch long and 3/4-inch wide. Make MARINADE, mix with pork and marinate 15 minutes or more.
2. Cut the green onion into 2-inch lengths, cut in half lengthwise and separate into thin shreds. Chop the garlic. Soak wood ear in warm water until softened, rinse well, cut away tough parts and cut into shreds.
3. Mix the SEASONINGS in a cup or small bowl.

TO COOK: 1. Heat 4 Tbsps. cooking oil in a *wok* or large frying pan until very hot. When the oil begins to smoke, add the

3–4 pieces wood ear
SEASONINGS
    1 Tbsp. soy sauce
    ½ tsp. salt
    2 tsps. vinegar
    2 tsps. sesame oil
4 Tbsps. oil

garlic, and a few seconds later add the pork (drain any excess MARINADE). Stir very quickly over the highest possible heat until the pork shreds turn white. (Speed is of the greatest importance here. If the heat is insufficient to cook the pork in 10–15 seconds, it is better to cook the pork a little at a time, removing the cooked pork to a bowl and then replacing all the meat in the *wok* before adding the wood ear, onion and SEASONINGS.)

2. Add the green onion, wood ear and SEASONINGS. Stir together until ingredients are well mixed and heated. Transfer to a serving dish and serve immediately.

Zha-cai Rou-si 榨菜肉絲
PORK SHREDS WITH SZECHWAN VEGETABLE

Szechwan vegetable is a very salty and somewhat hot pickled root-type vegetable, which some people don't particularly like or like only in small amounts. Replacing some of the Szechwan vegetable with bamboo shoot makes this recipe much milder, but even so, plan this dish with care.

½ lb. lean or slightly fatty pork
MARINADE
    2 tsps. rice wine or dry sherry
    1 Tbsp. soy sauce
1 large piece Szechwan vegetable, about equal or slightly less than the pork in bulk
bamboo shoot (optional—to be used in place of part of the Szechwan vegetable)
1 green onion
SEASONINGS
    2 tsps. rice wine or dry sherry
    2 tsps. soy sauce
    1 tsp. vinegar
    ½ tsp. sugar
4–6 Tbsps. cooking oil

TO PREPARE: 1. Slice pork thinly, then cut into shreds, about 1 to 1½-inches long and ¼-inch wide. Make MARINADE and marinate pork about 15 minutes.

2. Wash the reddish pickling material off the Szechwan vegetable and cut the vegetable into 1-inch-long shreds. Chop the bamboo shoot into 1-inch-long shreds. Chop the green onion into 1-inch lengths then into shreds.

3. Mix the SEASONINGS in a cup or small bowl.

TO COOK: 1. Heat 4–6 Tbsps. cooking oil in a *wok* or large frying pan over high heat. Drain any excess MARINADE from the meat, add the pork shreds and toss until pieces have turned gray.

2. Add the Szechwan vegetable, or bamboo shoot, and green onion and toss until all are heated. Add SEASONINGS, continue to stir-fry over high heat for a few more seconds, then remove to serving dish and serve hot.

La Zi Rou-ding

辣子肉丁

PORK WITH RED PEPPER (AND ZUCCHINI)

Somewhat hot, this pork recipe is prepared without garlic so its taste contrasts nicely with other spicier hot dishes. In China, huang-gua, a small green squash very similar to zucchini, is often used but bamboo shoot or water chestnuts may be substituted. You may also use other types of squash or whatever vegetable is in season.

½ lb. lean pork

MARINADE

    2 tsps. cornstarch mixed with 4 tsps. water

    1 egg white

    ½ tsp. salt

3–4 small zucchini, or bamboo shoot, water chestnuts, or another crisp vegetable

3–4 small fresh or dried red peppers

1 Tbsp. finely chopped fresh ginger

2 Tbsps. finely chopped green onion

2 tsps. hot bean sauce

½ tsp. salt

SEASONINGS

    2 tsps. cornstarch

    1 tsp. rice wine or dry sherry

    1 tsp. soy sauce

    ½ tsp. salt

    ½ tsp. sugar

2 tsps. sesame oil (optional)

approximately ⅔ cup oil

TO PREPARE: 1. Cut pork into small pieces, about ¾-inch in size. To make MARINADE, mix 2 tsps. cornstarch with 4 tsps. water to make a paste, and add salt and egg white. Mix with pork and marinate at least 10–15 minutes.

2. Wash the zucchini, cut into quarters lengthwise (or just halves if the zucchini is very small), and cut crosswise into small pieces. If using bamboo shoot, cut it into slices and then cut the slices into quarters. If using water chestnuts, slice into quarters. The idea is to make bite-sized pieces of whatever vegetable you are using.

3. If using dried red peppers, first soften them by soaking them in warm water. Then cut in half lengthwise and remove seeds with the tip of a knife. Cut the red peppers into small flakes. Chop ginger finely and cut green onion into ½-inch lengths.

4. Mix SEASONINGS in a cup or small bowl.

TO COOK: 1. Heat 4–6 Tbsps. cooking oil in a *wok* or large frying pan until the oil is hot. Add zucchini, or the vegetable of your choice, plus ½ tsp. salt. Toss until the vegetable pieces are covered with oil and heated. Remove and drain.

2. Heat 4–6 Tbsps. oil in the *wok* until the oil begins to smoke. Pour the excess marinade off the pork and add the meat to the *wok*. Toss quickly until the pieces of pork have turned white. Retaining the meat in the *wok*, pour off any excess oil, then add red peppers, green onion, ginger, hot bean sauce and prefried zucchini (or other vegetable ingredient). Toss over high heat until everything is well mixed and you can smell the hot bean sauce. Then add SEASONINGS (stir once before adding to the *wok*). Stir together over heat until everything is again well mixed and the sauce has thickened and begun to adhere to the pieces of pork and vegetable. If desired, sprinkle 2 tsps. sesame oil over the pork and zucchini and give everything a final stir. Remove to a serving dish and serve hot.

Ruan-zha Rou-pian
DEEP–FRIED TENDER PORK

軟炸肉片

Both the ingredients and the procedures for making Deep-fried Tender Pork are very simple. Not particularly Szechwanese cooking. Mild tasting.

½ lb. lean pork
MARINADE A
    2 tsps. rice wine or dry sherry
    1 tsp. salt
MARINADE B
    4 Tbsps. cornstarch mixed with ½ cup of water
    2 egg whites
SEASONINGS
    1–2 tsps. salt
    1–2 tsps. ground Szechwan pepper, or black pepper
oil for deep frying

TO PREPARE: 1. Cut the pork into thin slices about 1 to 1½-inches long. Using the back of the cleaver or a meat hammer, pound the pork slices until they are tender.

2. Make MARINADE A and mix with pork slices and marinate for 15 minutes or so. Then make MARINADE B by mixing the cornstarch with ½ cup water and beating this mixture into the egg whites. Mix thoroughly with the marinating pork slices.

3. Mix the SEASONINGS and arrange attractively in two small piles on opposite sides of a small platter or place in two small dishes.

TO COOK: 1. Heat 2–4 cups cooking oil in a *wok* or deep fryer. (The more oil you use, the more pork you can deep fry at one time. The left over oil can be used again. See page 30 for directions on how to reclaim oil.) Keep the oil at a high temperature but do not let it smoke excessively. Drain any excess MARINADE and, one at a time, add the pieces of sliced pork, keeping the pieces separate as they deep fry. Allow the pork slices to deep fry for about 12 seconds or until they turn gold. Then remove them with a slotted spoon and place in a side dish.

2. When all the pork slices have been deep fried once and allowed to cool slightly, replace all the pork in the *wok* and deep fry again for 5–10 seconds. Remove the pork slices and drain for a few moments. Arrange attractively on a serving plate between the small piles of pepper and salt and serve hot. Garnish with parsley.

Jiang Rou

醬 肉

PEKING–SAUCE–FLAVORED COLD PORK

Peking-sauce-flavored Cold Pork is to be served at room temperature. The star anise and dried orange peel make this easy-to-prepare dish a very special appetizer or main course.

1 lb. pork, loin or rump
3 Tbsps. sweet bean sauce
2 Tbsps. rice wine or dry sherry
½ cup soy sauce
3 pieces star anise
2 pieces dried or 1 piece fresh orange peel
2 green onions cut into 3-inch lengths
2 large slices fresh ginger

TO PREPARE: Clean pork and cut off any pieces that you won't want to eat. With a spatula, spread a thin layer of sweet bean sauce over the meat on all sides. Let stand 2 hours.

TO COOK: 1. Bring 3 cups of water to a boil in a *wok* or pot. Add the wine, soy sauce, star anise, dried orange peel, green onion, ginger and pork. Simmer over a low flame for about one hour, turning the meat occasionally. When the pork is tender, remove and cool. Discard other ingredients.
2. To serve, cut the cooled pork into thin slices or shreds and arrange on a serving platter. If desired, sprinkle with additional soy sauce. Garnish with parsley.

Sheng-bao Yan-jian Rou

生爆鹽煎肉

QUICKLY COOKED PORK WITH GREEN PEPPER

½ lb. lean pork, or a roast cut
1–2 green peppers, depending on size
1 Tbsp. finely chopped fresh ginger
1 Tbsp. finely chopped green onion
1 tsp. finely chopped garlic
½ tsp. salt
SEASONINGS
    1 Tbsp. rice wine or dry sherry
    2 tsps. soy sauce
    1 tsp. sugar
    2 tsps. sweet bean sauce
    1 Tbsp. hot bean sauce
2 tsps. sesame oil
approximately ¾ cup oil

TO PREPARE: 1. Slice pork thinly, then cut into shreds as small as 1-inch long and ⅛-inch wide if possible.
2. Top and remove seeds from green peppers and cut them into 1-inch sections. Chop ginger, garlic and green onion finely.
3. Mix the SEASONINGS in a cup or small bowl.

TO COOK: 1. Heat 6–8 Tbsps. cooking oil in a *wok* or large frying pan until the oil starts to smoke. Add the green pepper sections and ½ tsp. salt. Toss quickly until pieces of green pepper are coated with oil and heated. Remove and drain.
2. Heat another 6–8 Tbsps. cooking oil in the *wok* until the oil starts to smoke. Add the pork shreds (no marinade in this recipe.) Toss over the highest heat until shreds have cooked beyond the greyish-white stage and are beginning to turn gold. Add SEASONINGS, stir, then add the chopped ginger, green onion, garlic and prefried green pepper. Stir until everything is well mixed and heated, add sesame oil and stir once more. Remove to a serving dish and serve hot.

Yu-xiang Zhu-gan
PORK LIVER WITH YU–XIANG SAUCE

魚香猪肝

Somewhat hot and very spicy, this is an excellent way to cook liver, especially for people who don't ordinarily like liver. Its texture is completely different since the liver is cut into thin slices, and its normal taste is totally transformed. This dish can be adapted to beef and lamb liver very easily (see page 59), though I suggest you try pork liver at least once—it's undervalued in the West. For chicken liver, a somewhat milder version of yu-xiang sauce is given in the poultry section on page 58.

½ lb. pork liver
MARINADE
    2 tsps. cornstarch
    1 tsp. rice wine or dry sherry
    2 tsps. soy sauce
    ½ tsp. salt
1 Tbsp. finely chopped garlic
1 Tbsp. finely chopped fresh ginger
2–3 Tbsps. finely chopped green onion
4 water chestnuts
5–6 pieces wood ear (optional)
1 Tbsp. hot bean sauce
SEASONINGS
    2 tsps. cornstarch
    1 tsp. rice wine or dry sherry
    1 Tbsp. soy sauce
    1 tsp. salt
    ½–1 tsp. sugar
    1 tsp. vinegar
    2 tsps. sesame oil
½ cup oil

TO PREPARE: 1. Cut away any tough portions of the liver, and slice thinly, making about ¼-inch slices. Make MARINADE and mix with liver slices and marinate at least 10–15 minutes.
2. Chop the garlic, ginger, green onion and water chestnuts finely. Soak wood ear in warm water until softened, rinse well, cut away tough parts and cut into shreds.
3. In a cup or small bowl, mix the SEASONINGS, first mixing the cornstarch in the soy sauce and wine (or in 1 Tbsp. water) before adding the other ingredients.

TO COOK: 1. Heat 3 Tbsps. cooking oil in a *wok* or large frying pan until it starts to smoke. Drain any excess MARINADE from the liver and add the meat to the *wok*. Quickly toss liver over high heat until the meat turns gray. Remove and drain.
2. Heat 4 Tbsps. of cooking oil in the *wok*, add the hot bean sauce, then the garlic, ginger, green onion and water chestnuts. When these ingredients are will mixed and you can smell the garlic and the hot bean sauce, add the prefried liver and wood ear. Stir until the liver slices are coated with sauce. Then stir the SEASONINGS and add to the *wok*. Continue to toss over heat until everything is well mixed and the sauce is thickened. Remove to a serving platter and serve hot.

Chao Yao-hua

炒 腰 花

FRIED CHOPPED PORK KIDNEY WITH SNOW PEAS AND BAMBOO SHOOT

Kidneys are considered a delicacy in China as in other parts of the world. This recipe calls for the kidneys to be scored which facilitates cooking by creating more surface area. As they cook, the scored pieces of kidney will open slightly and are said to resemble flowers. Thus, the word hua, *or "flower," appears in the Chinese name.*

1 pair pork kidneys
¼ lb. snow peas
¼ cup bamboo shoot
5–8 pieces wood ear (optional)
2 green onions
1 Tbsp. finely chopped garlic
1 Tbsp. finely chopped fresh
  ginger
SEASONINGS
    2 tsps. cornstarch mixed
    with 3 Tbsps. water
    2 tsps. rice wine or dry
    sherry
    1 Tbsp. soy sauce
    1 tsp. salt
    ½ tsp. sugar
    1 tsp. vinegar
    2 tsps. sesame oil
4–6 Tbsps. oil

TO PREPARE: 1. Cut open the kidneys, cut away white tendons, and wash thoroughly. Score the surface of the kidneys with a sharp knife in a crosshatch pattern. Make the cuts about ½-inch (or less) apart and about ½-inch or so deep. Then cut the kidneys into pieces, 1-inch square or slightly smaller. 2. Cut off the ends of the snow peas. If desired, and especially if the snow peas are not absolutely tender and fresh, blanch them in boiling water. Drain the bamboo shoot and cut it into bite-sized slices. Soak wood ear in warm water until softened, rinse well, cut away tough parts and cut into shreds. Chop the green onion, garlic and ginger finely.
3. Mix the SEASONINGS, first mixing the cornstarch with 3 Tbsps. water before adding the other ingredients.

TO COOK: 1. Heat about a quart of water in a *wok* or pot until it boils. Add the kidney pieces and cook until the pieces have turned white. Remove and drain. Discard the water.
2. Heat 4–6 Tbsps. cooking oil in a *wok* or large frying pan. Add the green onion, garlic and ginger and toss until you can smell the garlic. Then add the bamboo shoot, snow peas and wood ear and toss until they are well heated and covered with oil. Next, add the parboiled kidneys and toss quickly until the kidneys are covered with oil and slightly heated. Immediately add SEASONINGS (stir once before adding to the *wok*) and continue to toss over medium heat for a few more moments until everything is mixed and heated. Transfer to a serving platter and serve hot.

Huo-bao Zhu-gan

火爆猪肝

FLASH–COOKED PORK LIVER WITH BAMBOO SHOOT OR WOOD EAR

This is another good liver dish but unlike Pork Liver with Yu-xiang Sauce (see page 75), it is not really hot. Instead of pork liver, beef or lamb liver can be substituted.

½ lb. pork liver thinly sliced

7–8 thin slices bamboo shoot, or 5–6 pieces wood ear

1 tsp. finely chopped fresh ginger

1 tsp. finely chopped garlic

1 Tbsp. finely chopped green onion

MARINADE

    2 tsps. cornstarch mixed with 1 Tbsp. water

    ½ tsp. black pepper

    2 tsps. rice wine or dry sherry

    ½ tsp. salt

SEASONINGS

    2 tsps. cornstarch

    2 tsps. rice wine or dry sherry

    2 tsps. soy sauce

    ½ tsp. salt

    1 tsp. sugar

2 tsps. sesame oil

½ tsp. ground Szechwan pepper

approximately ½ cup oil

TO PREPARE: 1. Cut away any tough portions of the liver and veins and slice thinly, making about ¼-inch slices. To make the MARINADE, mix the cornstarch with 1 Tbsp. water to make a paste and then add the black pepper, wine and salt. Mix with the liver and marinate at least 10–15 minutes.

2. Cut the bamboo shoot into thin bite-sized slices or if wood ear is to be used, soak the wood ear in warm water until softened, rinse well, cut away tough parts and cut into coarse shreds.

3. Chop the ginger, garlic and green onion finely.

4. Mix the SEASONINGS in a cup or small bowl, first mixing the cornstarch with the wine and soy sauce, then adding the salt and sugar.

TO COOK: 1. Heat ¼ cup cooking oil in a *wok* or large frying pan until very hot. Drain any excess MARINADE and add the pork liver to the oil and toss very rapidly over high heat until the liver is gray. Remove immediately and drain.

2. Heat 3–4 Tbsps. cooking oil in the *wok* until very hot. Add the bamboo shoot or wood ear and the ginger and green onion and cook until all are thoroughly heated. Then return the liver to the *wok* adding the garlic and SEASONINGS (stir once before adding to the *wok*). Toss briefly, then stir in the sesame oil. Remove to a serving dish and garnish with ground Szechwan pepper. Serve hot.

FISH AND SEAFOOD

Since the province of Szechwan is a great valley deep in western China, obviously there is no true "Szechwanese" cooking of seafood as such, though numerous dishes using Szechwanese techniques and seasonings have been adapted by restaurants or individuals in coastal areas. Szechwanese cooking does, however, make extensive use of freshwater fish—especially the many varieties of carp and several kinds of eel. Carp, a fish that is rarely eaten in the West, is rather bland and is usually prepared with highly flavored sauces. One may freely substitute almost any firm, white-fleshed fish in these recipes with reasonably good results. Catfish probably most closely approximates carp in flavor and texture.

Some of the seafood recipes in this section should be considered examples of northern or eastern Chinese cooking, but here the distinction scarcely matters. While local specialities exist, the general principles for preparing fish (and the numerous sauces) are broadly similar throughout northern and western China.

Fish are usually served whole—with head and tail—for aesthetic purposes and in most cases they are deep fried, with or without a batter. The head of the fish, especially the tender meat around the jowls, or cheeks, is considered a delicacy.

Cui-pi Chuan Yu

脆皮全魚

CRISPY-SKIN WHOLE FISH IN SWEET AND SOUR SAUCE

For many Westerners, Sweet and Sour Pork has become synonymous with Chinese cooking, but in fact, outside of Kwantung Province in southern China, this dish is not overwhelmingly popular. In northern and western China, sweet and sour sauce is more likely to be associated with fish, as in the recipe below. Use sea bass or another suitably sized firm, white-fleshed, saltwater or freshwater fish.

1½ lb. whole sea bass (a larger fish may be used but keep in mind that the fish has to be deep fried whole)

TO PREPARE: 1. Clean the fish—remove its entrails and scales, if necessary. Leave the head and tail intact. Make a series of fairly deep vertical cuts about 1-inch apart on both sides of the body.

MARINADE

> 4 Tbsps. rice wine or dry sherry
> 1 tsp. salt
> ½ tsp. black pepper

BATTER

> ½ cup cornstarch
> ½ cup water
> 2 eggs

2 green onions

3 Tbsps. finely chopped fresh ginger

2 tsps.–1 Tbsp. finely chopped garlic (optional)

SWEET AND SOUR SAUCE

> 3 Tbsps. sugar
> 3 Tbsps. vinegar
> 2 Tbsps. soy sauce
> 2 Tbsps. rice wine or dry sherry
> 4 Tbsps. ketchup
> 1 tsp. sesame oil
> 1 tsp. salt
> ½ tsp. black pepper
> ¼ cup water

1–2 tsps. cornstarch mixed with 2–4 tsps. water

oil for deep frying

2. Mix the MARINADE and apply it to both sides and the inside of the fish.

3. Make the BATTER by mixing the cornstarch with the water in a large bowl and then beating in the eggs. Place the fish in the bowl and roll it in the BATTER until it is thoroughly coated. The consistency of the BATTER should be thick enough to cling to the fish without running off, but not so thick that it adheres to the fish in large globules.

4. Chop the green onion, ginger and garlic finely.

5. Mix the ingredients for the SWEET AND SOUR SAUCE in a bowl.

TO COOK: 1. Heat several cups of cooking oil in a *wok* or deep fryer until very hot. Use enough cooking oil to cover at least half of the fish as it deep fries. Remove the fish from the BATTER, allowing the excess to drip off. Carefully lower the fish into the heated oil. Deep fry for 5–7 minutes, or until both sides are a deep golden brown. Turn the fish once, if necessary. Carefully remove to a serving platter.

2. Remove the oil from the *wok*. (For instructions on how to reclaim cooking oil, see page 30.)

3. Heat 4–6 Tbsps. cooking oil in the *wok* until very hot and add the green onion, ginger and garlic. Stir-fry briefly, just until the aroma of the green onion and ginger is noticeable. Then add the SWEET AND SOUR SAUCE. Bring to a boil, then reduce the heat and cook for a minute or so. Thicken the sauce by adding 1–2 tsps. of cornstarch mixed with 2–4 tsps. water. Pour over the fish and serve hot.

NOTE: Optional ingredients for the SWEET AND SOUR SAUCE: Shred ½ carrot, 1 small green pepper and ¼ cup bamboo shoot. In another *wok* or pan, stir-fry in a few Tbsps. heated cooking oil, first adding the carrots and stir-frying briefly and then adding the bamboo shoot and green pepper. Make sure all ingredients are heated and covered with oil and then remove to the *wok* or frying pan. Mix these vegetables with the SWEET AND SOUR SAUCE just before pouring it over the deep-fried fish (TO COOK: Step 3, above).

Xi-hu Yu

WESTERN–LAKE SOUR FISH

COLOR: page 39

西 湖 魚

Although the recipe calls for carp, the basic method of Western-Lake Sour Fish—poaching the fish and then garnishing it with fresh vegetables and a sweet and sour sauce—can be applied to any firm, white-fleshed fish.

1–1½ lb. whole carp
4 green onions
4 Tbsps. shredded fresh ginger
SEASONINGS
    ¼ cup soy sauce*
    2 Tbsps. rice wine or dry sherry
    1 tsp. sugar
    1 tsp. vinegar
    3 Tbsps. cornstarch mixed with 6 Tbsps. water
4–8 Tbsps. vegetable oil

*Reduce this amount if using heavy, strong Japanese-style soy sauce

TO PREPARE: 1. Clean the fish—remove its entrails and scales' if necessary. Rinse in cold water.
2. Cut the green onion into 2-inch lengths and then into shreds. Cut the ginger into shreds.
3. In a small bowl, mix the SEASONINGS, first mixing the cornstarch with the water and then adding the other ingredients.

TO COOK: 1. In a *wok* or a large frying pan or pot, bring to boil enough water to cover the fish. Place the fish in the boiling water and poach over medium heat until tender. Remove and drain and place on a serving platter.
2. Arrange the green onion and ginger shreds over the fish.
3. In the *wok*, retain only 2½ cups of the water used to poach the fish. Reheat the water and then add the SEASONINGS (stir once before adding to *wok*). Bring to a boil and then dribble 4–8 Tbsps. vegetable oil into the sauce, mixing thoroughly. Check for salt and richness and add more salt or vegetable oil to the sauce to taste. Pour over the fish and serve hot.

Dou-ban Yu

FISH WITH HOT SAUCE AND SPICES

豆 瓣 魚

1 whole, firm, white-fleshed fish, about 1 lb., or fish fillets
MARINADE
    2 Tbsps. rice wine or dry sherry
    2 Tbsps. soy sauce
1–3 green onions
1–2 Tbsps. finely chopped fresh ginger
1–2 Tbsps finely chopped garlic
1–2 Tbsps. hot bean sauce

TO PREPARE: 1. Clean the fish—remove its entrails and scales, if necessary. Wash thoroughly in cold water. Score the fish, making a series of vertical cuts, about ½-inch deep and ¾-inch apart, on both sides of the body. If using fillets, score lightly in the same fashion.
2. Mix the MARINADE and apply it to both sides and the inside of the fish.
3. Chop the green onion, ginger and garlic finely.
4. Mix the SEASONINGS in a cup or small bowl, first mixing the cornstarch with the water and then adding the other ingredients.

SEASONINGS

    2 tsps. cornstarch mixed
    with 4 tsps. water

    2 Tbsps. soy sauce

    3 Tbsps. rice wine or dry
    sherry

    $\frac{1}{2}$ tsp. salt

    1 tsp. sugar

    1 cup fish or chicken stock

$\frac{1}{2}$–1 cup oil

TO COOK: 1. Heat $\frac{1}{2}$ to 1 cup cooking oil in a *wok* or large frying pan until very hot. Drain any excess MARINADE, add the fish and deep fry on both sides until the fish has turned a deep brown and is tender. About 3–4 minutes on each side for a whole fish, but less time for fillets. Remove and drain and arrange on a serving platter. (For directions on how to reclaim cooking oil, see page 30.)

2. Retain only 4–6 Tbsps. of the cooking oil in the *wok*. Heat and then add the ginger and garlic and stir-fry briefly. Add the hot bean sauce and stir-fry briefly. Give the SEASONINGS a stir and add to the *wok*. Stir. Bring to a boil, then simmer briefly. Add the green onion and stir well. Pour the sauce over the fish and serve hot.

Cui-pi Gui-yu

脆皮桂魚

CRISPY–SKIN SALMON WITH SWEET AND SOUR SAUCE

Since the flavor of salmon is delicate, the sweet and sour sauce in this dish is relatively subdued. Rather than pouring the sauce over the fish, serve it in a separate bowl. The salmon is coated only with a thin layer of cornstarch-and-water mixture and then it is dusted with dry cornstarch.

1 whole fresh salmon, about 2 lbs.

MARINADE

    1 Tbsp. rice wine or dry
    sherry

    1 tsp. salt

    $\frac{1}{2}$ tsp. black pepper

2 Tbsps. finely chopped green onion

1 Tbsp. finely chopped fresh ginger

SEASONINGS

    3 Tbsps. ketchup

    2 Tbsps. sugar

    2 Tbsps. vinegar

    1 tsp. salt

2 Tbsps. cornstarch mixed with 3 Tbsps. water to make a paste

$\frac{1}{2}$ cup dry cornstarch

oil for deep frying

TO PREPARE: 1. Clean the salmon—remove its entrails and scales, if necessary. Wash thoroughly in cold water. Score the fish, making a series of curving cuts, about $\frac{1}{2}$-inch deep and about $\frac{3}{4}$ to 1-inch apart, vertically on both sides of the body.

2. Mix the MARINADE and apply it to both sides and the inside of the fish, especially rubbing it into the scores. Allow to stand at least 10 minutes.

3. Chop the green onions and ginger finely.

4. Mix the SEASONINGS in a cup.

TO COOK: 1. In a *wok* or deep fryer, heat several cupfuls of cooking oil, enough to deep fry the salmon. While the oil is heating, smear the thin paste of cornstarch and water over the surface of the salmon, then carefully dust the fish with the dry cornstarch. When the oil is hot, deep fry the salmon for 4–5 minutes on each side, or until it turns golden brown. Remove, drain and place on a serving platter. (For directions on how to reclaim cooking oil, see page 30.)

2. Heat 3–4 Tablespoons cooking oil in a *wok* or saucepan. Add the ginger and green onion and stir-fry briefly, 1–2 minutes. Add the SEASONINGS and stir. Let this liquid come to a boil, then simmer briefly, 1–2 minutes. Stir. Transfer to a small bowl and serve hot along with the deep-fried salmon.

Xun Yu

燻 魚

FRAGRANT FISH

Marinated in spices, deep fried and served at room temperature with a sweet and sour sauce, Fragrant Fish is one of the best known and most universally served fish dishes in China. The five spices called for in the recipe—a mixture of star anise, anise pepper, fennel, cloves and cinnamon—is sold ready-mixed and by weight at Chinese grocery stores. You may try substituting allspice or mixing equal amounts of powdered cinnamon, cloves, ginger and nutmeg.

1–1½ lbs. firm, white-fleshed fish fillets, halibut is excellent

MARINADE

    2 green onions

    2 Tbsps. finely chopped fresh ginger

    1 tsp. five spices

    5 Tbsps. soy sauce

    2 Tbsps. rice wine or dry sherry

    1 tsp. salt

1 cup water

2 Tbsps. sugar

SEASONINGS

    2 Tbsps. finely chopped green onion

    1 Tbsp. finely chopped fresh ginger

    2 tsps. sugar

    2 tsps. vinegar

    2 Tbsps. soy sauce

    ½ cup fish or chicken stock

    ½ tsp. five spices (optional)

approximately 1 cup oil

TO PREPARE: 1. Cut the fish fillets into slices across the grain. Finely chop the green onion and ginger that you will need for the MARINADE. Make the MARINADE and mix with the fish fillets and let marinate at least 2–3 hours.

2. Finely chop the green onion and ginger that you will need for the SEASONINGS. Mix the SEASONINGS in a small bowl.

TO COOK: 1. Bring a cup of water to boil in a small saucepan. Reduce the heat and add the 2 Tbsps. sugar, stirring until it is completely dissolved. Let simmer. Drain and save the excess MARINADE from the fish fillets.

2. On another burner, heat about 1 cup of cooking oil in a *wok* or large frying pan until very hot. Deep fry several pieces of fish until they are a golden brown. As soon as a piece is finished deep frying, drain it quickly and transfer it to the simmering sugar water. Leave in the syrup until just before you have to remove the next piece of fried fish from the *wok*. Continue this process until all the pieces of fish have been deep fried and then simmered in the sugar water. The fish slices should be allowed to fry for about 1 minute and then to simmer in the sugar water for about 1 minute.

3. Retain only 3 Tbsps. of cooking oil in the *wok* and discard the sugar water after completing the previous step. Heat the oil. Return the deep fried fish slices to the *wok* and fry briefly. Add the SEASONINGS and the remaining MARINADE (TO PREPARE: Step 2, above). Bring the sauce to a boil, then remove all the ingredients to a serving bowl. Serve when cool.

Cui-pi Wa-kuai Yu

脆皮瓦塊魚

CRISPY–SKIN BROKEN–TILE FISH

This dish—deep-fried fish fillets with a sweet and sour sauce—is very practical in terms of the kinds of fish that are most often available at American supermarkets. The sauce, a variation of the sweet and sour sauce so widely used in Chinese fish recipes, will make even the most anonymous fish fillet taste interesting. In this particular recipe, the sweet and sour flavor is subtle and the taste of green onion, garlic and sesame oil are more dominant.

1 lb. fish fillets*

MARINADE
   2 Tbsps. rice wine or dry sherry
   2 Tbsps. soy sauce
   1 tsp. salt

BATTER
   ½ cup flour
   ¼ cup cornstarch
   ½ cup cold water
   1 egg, or 2 duck eggs for the single chicken egg

1 green onion
1 Tbsp. finely chopped fresh ginger
1 Tbsp. finely chopped garlic

SEASONINGS
   2 tsps. cornstarch mixed with 4 tsps. water
   3 Tbsps. soy sauce
   2 Tbsps. rice wine or dry sherry
   1 Tbsp. vinegar
   2 tsps. sugar
   1 tsp. salt
   3 Tbsps. ketchup
   2 Tbsps. sesame oil
oil for deep frying

*In China, a type of carp would normally be used, but the fillets of any firm, white-fleshed fish are fine.

TO PREPARE: 1. Cut the fillets into 4 to 5-inch pieces of whatever shape.

2. Mix the MARINADE and sprinkle over the fish pieces.

3. Make the BATTER. In a medium-large bowl, combine and sift the cornstarch and flour then mix in the water and beat in the egg. The consistency of the BATTER should be thick and pastelike, but it may be necessary to thin it slightly by adding a few extra teaspoons of water. Add the fish pieces to the bowl and mix well, making sure that all the fish pieces are covered with BATTER.

4. Chop the green onion, ginger and garlic finely.

5. Mix the SEASONINGS in a small bowl, first mixing the cornstarch with the water and then adding the other ingredients.

TO COOK: 1. Heat several cups of cooking oil in a *wok* or deep fryer until very hot. Drain any excess MARINADE from the fish. Deep fry the fish pieces until they turn golden brown. Remove and drain.

2. Retain only 4–6 Tbsps. of the cooking oil in the *wok*. (For directions on how to reclaim cooking oil, see page 30.) Heat the oil and then add the green onion, ginger and garlic and stir-fry briefly. Return the deep-fried fish pieces to the *wok*, mixing them gently for 15–20 seconds.

3. Give the SEASONINGS a stir and then add to the *wok*. Stir well—quickly but gently (try to avoid breaking the fried fish pieces). As soon as the sauce is well mixed and heated, remove fish pieces and sauce to a serving dish and serve hot.

Hong-shao Man-yu

BRAISED EEL WITH BAMBOO SHOOT

COLOR: page 34

紅燒鰻魚

Similar recipes for preparing freshwater eel seem to be common throughout northern and western China. In this recipe, the seasoning is restrained and the taste mildly sweet.

1 lb. fresh eel
2–3 dried mushrooms
½ cup bamboo shoot
2 Tbsps. finely chopped green onion
2 tsps. finely chopped fresh ginger
2 Tbsps. rice wine or dry sherry
4–5 Tbsps. soy sauce
1 Tbsp. sugar dissolved in 2 cups water
salt, a pinch or so to taste
¼ tsp. black pepper
1 Tbsp. cornstarch mixed with 2 Tbsps. water
2 tsps. sesame oil
4–6 Tbsps. cooking oil

TO PREPARE: 1. Clean and remove the head and tail of each eel. To firm the eel flesh slightly, poach briefly in simmering water. Then remove the eel and carefully peel off its skin and bone it. Rinse in cold water and cut crosswise into 1-inch pieces.

2. Soak the dried mushroom in warm water until softened, cut away tough stems and cut into quarters or smaller pieces. Cut the bamboo shoot into thin, bite-sized slices. Chop the green onion and ginger fine.

TO COOK: 1. Heat 4–6 Tbsps. cooking oil in a *wok* or large frying pan until very hot. Add the green onion and ginger. Stir-fry over medium-high or high heat until the aroma of the onion and ginger is noticeable. Then add the pieces of eel. Stir gently until all the pieces have been coated with oil, then turn down the heat.

2. Stir in the wine. Mix well, adding the soy sauce and the sugar dissolved in 2 cups water, salt, black pepper, the mushrooms and bamboo shoot. Stir well. Bring to a boil, then turn the fire down very low and gently simmer until the liquid has almost boiled away. Add the cornstarch having first mixed it with the water. Stir. Then add the sesame oil. (If you prefer something juicier, add 1 or 2 Tbsps. more cooking oil.) Stir. Check for salt. Mix well, taking great care not to break the delicate pieces of eel. Remove to a serving bowl and serve hot.

Shan-hu Yu

CORAL FISH

珊瑚魚

1 lb. perch, or firm-fleshed freshwater fish or fillets
MARINADE
    ½ tsp. salt
    2 tsps. rice wine or dry sherry

TO PREPARE: 1. Remove the fish head and tail (use these to make fish stock, see page 115) and clean and scale the fish. Cut through the body crosswise, through the spine, making 1-inch wide steaks. Make the MARINADE and mix with the fish pieces and marinate at least 10–20 minutes.

2. Shred the bamboo shoot, leek and ginger. Cut off the top

½ cup bamboo shoot

2 Tbsps. shredded leek or green onion

1 Tbsp. shredded fresh ginger

4–5 shredded fresh or dried red peppers

SEASONINGS

    2 tsps. rice wine or dry sherry

    1 tsp. sugar

    1 tsp. salt

    2 cups fish or chicken stock

2 tsps. red oil

½ cup oil

4 Tbsps. sesame oil

of the red peppers and shake out the seeds. Cut into shreds. If using dried red peppers, soak in warm water until softened, then top, seed, and shred them.

3. Mix the SEASONINGS in a small bowl.

To COOK: 1. Heat ½ cup cooking oil in a *wok* or large frying pan until very hot. Drain any excess MARINADE from the fish. Add the fish pieces a few at a time, deep frying until lightly browned. Remove and drain. Repeat this process until all the fish pieces have been deep fried, then empty the *wok* of oil. (For directions on how to reclaim cooking oil, see page 30.) 2. Heat 4 Tbsps. sesame oil in the *wok* until very hot, but do not let it burn. Add the red peppers, ginger, leek and bamboo shoot shreds and stir-fry these ingredients for about 1 minute. 3. Add the SEASONINGS and stir. Add the deep fried fish pieces. Bring to a boil then reduce the heat and simmer until the liquid has been reduced and has almost cooked away. Stir in the red oil. Remove to a serving dish and serve hot.

Jiao-ma Yu

椒麻魚

FISH WITH JIAO-MA SAUCE

This way of preparing fish, particularly common in Pekinese cooking, is good for small, bony fish like perch or sunfish because the bones of the fish become quite soft during the cooking process. This method may also be applied to fillets of larger fish though extra care must be taken not to break the flesh. The jiao-ma sauce blends the taste of Szechwan pepper and sesame.

1 lb. of whole perch or sunfish, or other small whole white-fleshed fish or fillets of larger white-fleshed fish

MARINADE

    2 tsps. rice wine or dry sherry

    1 tsp. salt

¼–½ cup finely chopped leek or green onion

3 Tbsps. finely chopped green onion

2 thin slices fresh ginger

To PREPARE: 1. Clean the fish—remove entrails and scales, if necessary. Cut off the heads and tails. Cut through the backbone and cut the meat into 1-inch or 3-inch sections, depending on the width of the fish. If using fillets, cut the meat into 2-inch pieces.

2. Make the MARINADE and mix with the fish pieces.

3. Chop the leek or green onion and the ginger finely.

4. Mix the SEASONINGS in a small bowl.

To COOK: 1. Heat ½ cup of the cooking oil in a *wok* or large frying pan until very hot. Add the fish pieces, frying them until they turn golden brown. Remove and drain. (For directions on how to reclaim cooking oil, see page 30.)

2. Heat a dry *wok* and add the 4 Tbsps. sesame oil and sugar.

    $\frac{1}{2}$ tsp. ground Szechwan pepper

    1 tsp. rice wine or dry sherry

    $1\frac{1}{2}$ cups fish or chicken stock

    $\frac{1}{2}$ tsp. salt

    1 Tbsp. sugar

1 Tbsp. sugar

$\frac{1}{4}$ tsp. ground Szechwan pepper

$\frac{1}{2}$ cup oil

$4\frac{1}{2}$ Tbsps. sesame oil

Stir over a low fire for several minutes and then add the $\frac{1}{4}$–$\frac{1}{2}$ cup chopped leek or green onion, ginger and the SEASONINGS. Stir well.

3. Return the fried fish pieces to the *wok*. Simmer until most of the liquid has disappeared, then add the $\frac{1}{4}$ tsp. ground Szechwan pepper, the 3 Tbsps. chopped green onion and the remaining $\frac{1}{2}$ Tbsp. sesame oil. Stir together, remove to a serving dish and serve hot.

Cong-kao Yu 葱烤魚
FRESHWATER FISH AND GREEN ONION

1 lb. whole carp or catfish, or other firm, white-fleshed freshwater fish

MARINADE

    2 Tbsps. rice wine or dry sherry

    2 Tbsps. soy sauce

3–4 green onions

SEASONINGS

    2 Tbsps. rice wine or dry sherry

    2 Tbsps. soy sauce

    2 tsps. sugar

    $\frac{1}{2}$ cup fish or chicken stock

1 tsp. vinegar

1 tsp. sesame oil

$\frac{1}{2}$ cup oil

TO PREPARE: 1. Clean the fish—remove its entrails and scales, if necessary. Leave the head and tail intact. Score the fish, making vertical cuts about $\frac{1}{2}$-inch deep, $\frac{3}{4}$-inch apart, on both sides of the body.

2. Mix the MARINADE and apply it to both sides and the inside of the fish.

3. Cut the green onion into 1-inch lengths. Mix the SEASONINGS in a small bowl.

TO COOK: 1. Heat $\frac{1}{2}$ cup cooking oil in a *wok* or large frying pan until a haze forms above the oil. Place the fish in the heated oil and fry on both sides until the fish turns a golden yellow. (This does not mean brown.) Remove and drain.

2. Retain only 4–6 Tbsps. of the cooking oil in the *wok*. Heat the oil and then add the green onion lengths and stir-fry for about 45 seconds.

3. Place the fried fish in the *wok* on top of the green onion and pour the SEASONINGS over both. Cover the *wok* (invert a large earthenware bowl over the *wok* if you don't have a suitable cover). Turn the flame as low as possible and simmer for about 20 minutes. If the liquid appears to be boiling away add more stock or water as needed.

4. Carefully remove the fish to a serving platter. With a slotted spoon, remove the green onions from the *wok* and

arrange attractively over and around the fish. Cook down the liquids remaining in the *wok* over a higher flame until they thicken. Stir in the vinegar and sesame oil. Pour the sauce over the fish and green onion and serve hot.

Gong-bao Xia-ren
公保蝦仁
SHRIMP WITH CHARRED RED PEPPERS

This recipe is an adaptation of the well-known chicken dish Gong-bao Ji Ding *(see page 45). Slightly hot but may be made hotter by using more dried red peppers, up to eight or ten.*

³⁄₄ lb. cleaned fresh shrimp
I cup cold water
¹⁄₂ tsp. salt
MARINADE
    2 tsps. cornstarch mixed with 4 tsps. water
    ¹⁄₂ egg white
    ¹⁄₂ tsp. salt
2 tsps. finely chopped green onion
I tsp. finely chopped fresh ginger
I tsp. finely chopped garlic
4 dried red peppers, or increase this number to as many as 8 to 10
SEASONINGS
    I tsp. cornstarch mixed with 2 tsps. water
    I¹⁄₂ Tbsp. soy sauce
    I tsp. vinegar
    2 tsp. rice wine or dry sherry
    ¹⁄₂ tsp. sugar
    ¹⁄₂ tsp. salt
    ¹⁄₄ tsp. black pepper
approximately 6 Tbsps. oil

TO PREPARE: I. Shell and devein the shrimp. Place in a bowl and add ¹⁄₂ tsp. salt and I cup cold water. Allow to stand 2 minutes, then rinse with cold water about I minute, or until the shrimp start to turn slightly white.
2. Make the MARINADE by mixing the cornstarch with the water and then beating in the egg white and the salt. Mix with the shrimp and allow to stand at least 20 minutes.
3. Chop the green onion, ginger and garlic finely. Cut off the tops of the dried red peppers and shake out the seeds.
4. Mix the SEASONINGS in a cup or small bowl, first mixing the cornstarch with the water and then adding the other ingredients.

TO COOK: I. Heat 3–4 Tbsps. of the cooking oil in a *wok* or large frying pan over a high heat. Drain any excess MARINADE, add the shrimp and stir-fry only 8–10 seconds. The shrimp should curl up. Remove immediately and drain.
2. Add more cooking oil to the *wok* to equal 4 Tbsps., or slightly more. Heat the oil and add the whole dried red peppers and fry over medium-high heat until the peppers begin to char and are almost black. (It is best to open the kitchen windows wide while stir-frying the dried red peppers.)
3. Add the green onion, ginger and garlic and stir-fry briefly. (By this time the peppers should be completely blackened.) Return the stir-fried shrimp to the *wok*, stir quickly, then give the SEASONINGS a stir and mix in with the other ingredients. Stir quickly, remove to a serving dish and serve hot.

Gan-shao Xia-ren

BRAISED SHRIMP

乾燒蝦仁

¾ lb. cleaned fresh shrimp
1 tsp. finely chopped ginger
2 tsps. finely chopped green onion
1 fresh or dried red pepper
1–2 tsps. hot bean sauce
1 tsp. salt
½ tsp. black pepper
1½ cups fish or chicken stock
2 tsps. rice wine or dry sherry
2–3 Tbsps. ketchup
2 tsps. cornstarch mixed with 4 tsps. water
1 tsp. sesame oil
approximately ⅔ cup oil

To PREPARE: 1. Shell and devein the shrimp. Wash thoroughly in cold water. If the shrimps are large, you may cut each into thirds or quarters.

2. Chop the green onions and ginger finely. Cut the top off the red pepper, shake out the seeds and cut into shreds or chop finely. If using dried red pepper, soak in warm water until softened and then seed and shred it.

To COOK: 1. Heat 4 Tbsps. of the cooking oil in a *wok* or small frying pan until very hot. Add the hot bean sauce, red pepper, ginger, green onion and salt and pepper. Stir-fry briefly, then remove to a bowl.

2. Heat 4–6 Tbsps. of the cooking oil in the *wok* or large frying pan until very hot and add the shrimp and stir-fry for a few moments. Immediately add the stock and wine. Stir.

3. Turn the fire down as low as possible, add the previously fried ingredients (To COOK: Step 1, above) and simmer for several minutes, or until the liquid has almost disappeared. Add the ketchup and the cornstarch mixed with water to thicken the sauce. (It may not be necessary to use all the cornstarch-water mixture.) Sprinkle the sesame oil over the dish and stir. Remove to a serving dish and serve hot.

Gan-bei Ya-cai

DRIED SCALLOPS AND BEAN SPROUTS

干貝芽菜

3–5 dried scallops, or fresh or canned scallops (which produce good or even better results)
¾ lb. bean sprouts
1½ tsps. salt
½ tsp. sugar
½ tsp. vinegar
2 tsps. sesame oil
½ cup cooking oil

To PREPARE: 1. Wash the dried scallops, place them in warm water and allow to soak about two hours. (Omit this step if using fresh or canned scallops.)

2. Drain and place scallops on a heat-proof dish in a steamer. Steam until tender, about 20 minutes. Remove and cool. Then, use your fingers to tear the scallops into fine shreds.

3. Wash the bean sprouts and, if desired, remove their dark ends. Drain.

To COOK: 1. Heat ½ cup cooking oil in a *wok* or large frying pan over a medium fire until hot. Add the scallop shreds and deep fry, stirring, until the shreds turn a golden brown. Remove and drain and sprinkle with ½ tsp. of the salt.

2. Leave only 4–6 Tbsps. of the cooking oil in the *wok*. (For instructions on how to reclaim cooking oil, see page 30.) Heat over a high flame and add the bean sprouts, sugar, vinegar and the remaining 1 tsp. of salt. Stir-fry for 1–2 minutes, or until the bean sprouts are well heated. Add the sesame oil, stir, and remove to a serving plate. Sprinkle the deep-fried scallop shreds on top of the bean sprouts and serve hot.

Zha-sheng Hao
DEEP–FRIED OYSTERS

炸生蠔

¾ lb. shelled fresh oysters
BATTER
    6 Tbsps. flour
    3 Tbsps. cornstarch
    6 Tbsps. cold water
    2 tsps. salt
    2 Tbsps. vegetable oil
SEASONINGS
    2 tsps. salt
    1 tsp. ground Szechwan pepper
oil for deep frying

To PREPARE: 1. Wash the shelled oysters, removing any extraneous pieces of shell.

2. Bring several cups of water to boil in a *wok* or pot. Using a large wire spoon or colander, dip the oysters into the boiling water and parboil for 30 seconds or so. Remove immediately and drain. Discard the water.

3. To make the BATTER, sift the flour and cornstarch together. In a medium-large bowl, combine this mixture and the water and then stir in the salt and vegetable oil. Add the parboiled oysters to the BATTER and mix thoroughly.

4. Mix the SEASONINGS in a cup.

To COOK: 1. Heat several cups of cooking oil in a *wok* or deep fryer until very hot. Then reduce the heat to medium. Using chopsticks, remove the oysters from the BATTER and deep fry one by one. Fry each oyster in the heated oil until it turns golden brown. Make sure that the cooking oil is not too hot, otherwise the BATTER will brown quickly but the oysters will be underdone. As each oyster is deep fried, drain briefly; then transfer to a serving platter. (For directions on how to reclaim cooking oil, see page 30.)

2. Serve with the SEASONINGS arranged in two piles on either end of the platter. Garnish with parsley and lemon.

Jiang-bao Qing-xie
FRESH CRAB WITH PEKING SAUCE

醬爆青蟹

½–¾ lb. fresh hard-shell crab, or crab legs

2 tsps. finely chopped fresh ginger

1 tsp. finely chopped green onion

1 Tbsp. sweet bean sauce mixed with 1 Tbsp. water

½ cup fish or chicken stock

2 tsps. rice wine or dry sherry

1 tsp. salt

½ tsp. sugar

2 tsps. soy sauce

2 tsps. cornstarch mixed with 2 tsps. water

½–1 cup oil

TO PREPARE: 1. If desired, parboil the crab in boiling water for a minute or so before dismembering it. Crack open the shell of the crab, clean and remove the entrails. Wash thoroughly in cold water. Detach the claws and legs. Discard the lower part of the legs and crack the shells of the claws and legs but do not remove the meat. Using a cleaver, cut the body of the crab in half from front to back. Then cut each half into several pieces. Do not remove the meat from the shell.

2. Chop the green onion and ginger finely. Mix the sweet bean sauce with the water. Mix the cornstarch with the water. Have the other ingredients on hand.

TO COOK: 1. Heat ½ to 1 cup cooking oil in a *wok* or large frying pan over a medium-high flame. Add the crab pieces and deep fry, stirring, for 15–20 seconds. Remove and drain.

2. Leave only 4–6 Tbsps. of the cooking oil in the *wok*. (For instructions in how to reclaim cooking oil, See page 30.) Heat the oil over a medium flame, then add the green onion and ginger. Stir-fry briefly, then return the deep-fried crab to the *wok*. Stir-fry for a few moments.

3. Add the stock, wine and salt. Stir well for a few seconds, then pull the crab pieces up from the center of the *wok* onto the sides. Add sweet bean sauce-water, sugar and soy sauce to the liquid in the bottom of the *wok*. Stir well, then let the pieces of crab return to the bottom of the *wok*. Stir.

4. Give the cornstarch and water mixture a stir and then add this to the contents of the *wok*. Stir over heat until the sauce thickens and adheres to the crab pieces. Remove to a serving dish and serve hot.

VEGETABLES AND DOU-FU

This section has been intentionally limited to dishes which are reasonably well known or require special techniques. Since many of the so-called meat dishes contain vegetables, this category is further restricted to those dishes which principally, if not exclusively, consist of vegetables. Obviously, any fresh vegetable may be stir-fried in a bit of cooking oil and served as a course at a Chinese meal. The following section includes simple recipes of this type, for example Quick-fried Fresh Spinach and Fried Celery.

Dou-fu, or bean curd, is a high-protein food made from soy beans and is very commonly seen as a main dish on Chinese tables. A good meat substitute, dou-fu is sold in soft cakes or blocks at Chinese grocery stores and sometimes at health food stores.

Chao Jie-cai   炒 芹 菜
FRIED CELERY

This is an example of how to cook firm green vegetables. You can apply this basic procedure to fresh asparagus, snow peas (in this case omit the green onion and Szechwan pepper), Swiss chard, green beans, and so on. If you like, add a few drops of sesame oil for flavoring just before serving.

1 lb. celery
5–8 Szechwan peppercorns
2 Tbsps. finely chopped green
  onion
SEASONINGS
    2 tsps. rice wine or dry
    sherry
    1–2 Tbsps. soy sauce
    1 tsp. sugar
    ½–1 tsp. salt ← omit
4–6 Tbsps. oil

TO PREPARE: 1. Wash and clean the celery. Remove the base and cut off the leafy top. If desired, remove the strings. Cut the celery into ¾-inch lengths. Chop the green onion finely.
2. Mix the SEASONINGS in a cup or small bowl.

TO COOK: 1. Heat 4–6 Tbsps. cooking oil in a *wok* or large frying pan until very hot. Add the Szechwan peppercorns and fry for 15–20 seconds. Remove and discard the peppercorns, using a spoon, fine wire mesh or spatula. If you decide to leave the peppercorns in the dish, be careful not to eat them— they are for flavoring the cooking oil only.
2. Add the green onion and stir-fry briefly. Add the celery pieces and stir-fry for up to 1 minute. Add the SEASONINGS. Stir-fry briefly, remove to a serving dish and serve hot.

Yu-xiang Qie-bing

魚香茄餅

STUFFED DEEP-FRIED EGGPLANT ROLLS WITH YU-XIANG SAUCE

4–6 small Asian-type egg-plants, or about 1 lb. large ones

½ lb. commercially ground or finely chopped pork, or a combination of pork and beef

6–7 Tbsps. finely chopped green onion

3 Tbsps. finely chopped fresh ginger

2–4 Tbsps. finely chopped garlic

2 water chestnuts (optional)

1 tsp. salt

1 Tbsp. cornstarch mixed with 2 Tbsps. water or soy sauce

1–2 Tbsps. hot bean sauce

BATTER

    1 Tbsp. cornstarch

    2 tsps. flour

    2 Tbsps. water

    ½ tsp. salt

    2 eggs

SEASONINGS

    4½ tsps.–2 Tbsps. soy sauce

    1 tsp. vinegar

    ½ tsp. sugar

    ½ tsp. ground Szechwan pepper (optional)

2 tsps. cornstarch mixed with 4 tsps. water

2 tsps. sesame oil

1¼ cups oil

TO PREPARE: 1. Peel the skin off the eggplants and cut them in half lengthwise. If you are using large eggplants, quarter them. With a small knife or the tip of a cleaver, hollow out each eggplant half slightly. Sprinkle with a little salt and let stand as you complete TO PREPARE: Steps 2 and 3, below.

2. If using commercially ground meat, break the meat down with a fork. Otherwise, finely chop the pork. Chop the green onion, ginger and garlic finely. Chop the water chestnuts very finely.

3. Thoroughly mix the chopped pork with 3–4 Tbsps. of the green onion, 3 Tbsps. of the ginger, the 1 tsp. salt and the 1 Tbsp. cornstarch, first having mixed it with 2 Tbsps. water or soy sauce.

4. Pat the eggplant dry. (The salt that was sprinkled over them should draw water out of the vegetable.) Estimate how much meat mixture you will need to stuff each eggplant half, then press a small amount of the meat mixture into the depression in each of the hollowed-out eggplant halves. Use all the meat mixture.

5. In a small bowl, make the BATTER by first mixing the corn-starch and flour with the water. Add the salt and beat in the eggs. Mix thoroughly.

6. Mix the SEASONINGS in a cup or small bowl.

TO COOK: 1. Heat 1¼ cups cooking oil in a *wok* or deep fryer until very hot, almost to the point of smoking. One by one, dip or roll each meat-filled eggplant half in the BATTER and then deep fry each separately until it turns a golden color. Remove and drain.

2. When all the eggplant halves have been deep fried, empty the *wok* and clean it. (For instructions on how to reclaim cooking oil, see page 30.) Heat 2 Tbsps. of the remaining cooking oil in the *wok* until very hot. Add the hot bean sauce, garlic, water chestnuts, and the remaining 2 Tbsps. chopped ginger and 3 Tbsps. green onion. Stir-fry. When the aroma becomes pronounced, carefully add the deep-fried eggplant halves and SEASONINGS. Stir briefly, being careful not to break the eggplant halves.

3. Add the 2 tsps. cornstarch, first having mixed it with 4 tsps. water. Stir carefully. Finally sprinkle the sesame oil over the eggplant rolls and sauce. Check for salt. Remove to a serving dish and serve hot.

Yu-xiang qie-zi

魚香茄子

EGGPLANT WITH YU-XIANG SAUCE

COLOR: page 36

This eggplant recipe is one of the best of all Szechwanese dishes. It is also very inexpensive when eggplant is in season. Somewhat hot, this dish tastes best when the garlic is literally overpowering. If you don't peel the eggplant, the color of this dish will be purplish.

1–2 large eggplants or 4–8 small Asian-type eggplants, about 1 lb.

¼ lb. pork

2 green onions

2–3 Tbsps. finely chopped fresh ginger

3–5 Tbsps. finely chopped garlic (a handful is the right attitude here)

1 Tbsp. hot bean sauce, or more depending on how hot a dish you want

SEASONINGS
  2 Tbsps. soy sauce
  1 tsp. salt
  1 tsp. sugar
  ½ cup chicken or pork stock or water

2 tsps. sesame oil

1 Tbsp. cornstarch mixed with 2 Tbsps. water

approximately ¾ cup oil

TO PREPARE: 1. If you like the taste and texture of the eggplant skin, begin making this dish by washing the eggplant and cutting it into strips about 3-inches long and as thick as your little finger. If you don't like the skin, cut it off before cutting the eggplant into strips. Salt them lightly, and pat dry in 5 or 10 minutes.

2. Chop the pork meat into small, ¼-inch pieces. Chop the green onion into small pieces. Chop the fresh ginger and garlic as finely as possible.

3. Mix the SEASONINGS in a small bowl.

TO COOK: 1. Heat ½ cup of the cooking oil in a *wok* or large frying pan until very hot. Add the eggplant and then turn the flame down to medium. Cook, stirring frequently, until the eggplant strips have become soft and moist looking. The eggplants will absorb a lot of oil so you may have to add more cooking oil as they cook. Remove them from the *wok* with a slotted spoon and drain. Press the excess oil out of the eggplant with a spoon or spatual. (This step can be done ahead of time and the eggplant set aside until you want to finish making the rest of the dish.)

2. Heat 3 Tbsps. of the cooking oil in the *wok* until very hot. Add the meat pieces and stir-fry briefly until the pork is gray. Then add the ginger, garlic and hot bean sauce. Cook, stirring, until the ginger, garlic and meat begin to absorb the red color from the hot bean sauce. Add the SEASONINGS. Stir briefly, then add the precooked eggplant strips.

3. Cook, stirring occasionally, until the liquid starts to disappear. Add the green onion and sesame oil. Stir and add the cornstarch mixed with a small amount of water. Stir. When the sauce has thickened and begins to adhere to the eggplant strips, remove to a serving dish and serve hot.

93

Ban Qie-ni
"PUREED" EGGPLANT WITH SESAME PASTE

拌茄泥

This dish is very unusual and rarely finds its way to Chinese-American restaurant menus. Said to be currently popular in Peking.

½ lb. eggplant
2 tsps. finely chopped garlic
½–1 tsp. finely chopped fresh
    or dried coriander leaves
1 tsp. finely chopped fresh
    celery leaves
1 Tbsp. sesame paste
1 tsp. salt
2 tsps. sesame oil

To COOK AND SERVE: 1. Slice off the ends of the eggplant and peel off the skin. Cut the eggplant into very thin slices. Wash and drain and arrange the eggplant slices on a heat-proof dish in a steamer and steam for 20–30 minutes, or until the slices become very soft. (See page 22 for directions on how to improvise a steamer.) Remove and cool.
2. Chop the garlic very finely or put it through a garlic press. Chop the fresh coriander and fresh celery leaves very fine.
3. Mix together the cooled eggplant slices, garlic, coriander, celery leaves, sesame paste, salt and sesame oil. Stir vigorously, or beat it, until all the ingredients are well mixed and the eggplant slices have broken up completely. Transfer to a serving bowl and serve at room temperature.

Sheng-bian Buo-cai
QUICK–FRIED FRESH SPINACH

生煸菠菜

This recipe gives you an idea of how to prepare leafy green vegetables. You can add meat, for example pork, beef or liver, to this or any other so-called vegetable dish. Cut the meat into thin bite-sized pieces or shreds and stir-fry before adding the spinach. Increase the amount of cooking oil by one or two tablespoons.

¾–1 lb. fresh spinach
SEASONINGS
    1 tsp. rice wine or dry
    sherry
    ½ tsp. vinegar
    2 tsps. soy sauce
    2 tsps. sugar
    1 tsp. salt
1 tsp. sesame oil or vegetable oil
6 Tbsps. oil

To PREPARE: 1. Wash the spinach thoroughly and drain. Separate the leaves and discard any discolored ones.
2. Mix the SEASONINGS in a cup or small bowl.

To COOK: 1. Heat 6 Tbsps. cooking oil in a *wok* or large frying pan until very hot. Add the spinach leaves and stir-fry for about 1 minute.
2. Add the SEASONINGS and stir. Add the sesame oil. Stir briefly. Remove to a serving dish and serve hot.

Gan-bian Si-ji-dou

DRY–FRIED STRING BEANS

乾煸四季豆

COLOR: page 38

Occasionally you may see "four-season beans" (si-ji dou, 四季豆) in a Chinese grocery store. They are longer than Western string, or French, beans but their taste is similar. If available, use them in this recipe. In making this dish, the green beans are first deep fried, then cooked with pork, Szechwan vegetable, dried shrimp and green onion. The result is very unusual for there is no sauce to speak of. Substitute bacon for pork in this recipe—the smoky flavor of bacon doesn't seem at all out of place.

1–1½ lbs. fresh "four season beans" or green beans

3–4 dried shrimp

2 Tbsps. finely chopped Szechwan vegetable

¼ lb. pork

2 Tbsps. finely chopped green onion

SEASONINGS

    2–3 Tbsps. soy sauce

    2–3 Tbsps. rice wine or dry sherry

    1½ tsps. sugar

    1 tsp. salt

    3 Tbsps. water

    2–3 Tbsps. sesame oil

½–1 cup oil

TO PREPARE: 1. Wash the green beans, drain, pat dry, cut off the ends and remove strings. Cut into 2 or 3-inch lengths.

2. Chop shrimp finely. Wash the red pickling material off the Szechwan vegetable and chop the vegetable finely. Chop the pork meat and green onion finely.

3. Mix the SEASONINGS in a small bowl.

TO COOK: 1. Heat about ½–1 cup cooking oil in a *wok* or large frying pan until very hot. Add the green beans, only one handful at a time. Deep fry until the skin of the green beans becomes crackled and wrinkled and the beans darken and become soft. When each batch has deep fried, remove it from the *wok* with a slotted spoon and drain. Allow the oil to reheat between batches if necessary.

2. When all the green beans have been deep fried, remove all but 2–3 Tbsps. of the cooking oil from the *wok*. (For instructions on how to reclaim cooking oil, see page 30.) Heat these few tablespoons cooking oil over high heat and add the finely chopped pork. Stir-fry until the pork is well cooked, or past the white-colored stage, and is beginning to brown.

3. Then add the chopped Szechwan vegetable and chopped dried shrimp. Toss together over high heat until these ingredients are thoroughly heated.

4. Add the prefried green beans. Continue to toss until the green beans are reheated. Then add the SEASONINGS. Stir.

5. Add the finely chopped green onion. Continue to cook over high heat until the liquid has almost disappeared. At this stage of preparation, all the chopped ingredients should be well distributed through the dish, adhering slightly to the beans. (If this is not the case, add a very small amount of cornstarch mixed with a little water at this time and stir it well.) Transfer to a serving dish and serve hot.

Ma-po Dou-fu

麻婆豆腐

COLOR: page 40

Mao-po Dou-fu is more correctly but less frequently called Chen Ma-po Dou-fu, *or "Old Pockmarked Mrs. Chen's Bean Curd." It takes its name from the wife of a certain Ch'en Fu-chih who ran a restaurant in the large provincial town of Chengtu in Szechwan in the 1860s. A very well-known Szechwanese dish,* Ma-po Dou-fu *should be very hot. Variations of this popular dish are numerous—some restaurants prepare it using garlic and ginger, some cooks replace the pork with beef, some recipes call for fermented black beans. The recipe I have included has been called "the authentic and original Ma-po Dou-fu," but you can take that statement as seriously as you like.* Ma-po Dou-fu *should be eaten not just with, but on top of, rice. Provide a serving spoon and let each person take a helping from the serving bowl and transfer it to his rice bowl before eating.*

3–4 cups cubed bean curd, about 1½ Japanese-style bean curd cakes or 3–4 smaller Chinese-style cakes

⅓–½ lb. fatty pork

3–5 Tbsps. finely chopped fresh ginger

¼ cup coarsely chopped green onion

1–2 Tbsps. hot bean sauce

1 cup pork or chicken stock or water

SEASONINGS

  2–3 Tbsps. cornstarch mixed with 4–6 Tbsps. water

  1–2 tsps. salt, depending on the saltiness of the hot bean sauce

  1 Tbsp. rice wine or dry sherry

  1 Tbsp. soy sauce

½ tsp. ground Szechwan pepper

4–5 Tbsps. cooking oil

OPTIONAL

2 Tbsps. finely chopped garlic

1 tsp. fermented black beans

2–3 dried or fresh mushrooms

6–8 pieces wood ear

1 Tbsps. sesame oil

TO PREPARE: 1. Cut the bean curd into small cubes. If desired, place the bean curd in boiling water in a *wok* or pot and let boil until the bean curd starts to float. This procedure firms the bean curd slightly and is especially advisable if you are using soft, Japanese-style bean curd.

2. Chop the pork into small pieces, about ¼-inch by ¼-inch, or slightly smaller. Chop the green onion coarsely. Chop the ginger as finely as possible.

3. Mix the SEASONINGS in a cup, first dissolving the cornstarch in the water and then adding the other ingredients.

TO COOK: 1. Heat 4–5 Tbsps. cooking oil in a *wok* or large frying pan until very hot. (The recipe actually calls for rendered pork fat but I invariably use vegetable oil and fatty pork instead.) Add the pork pieces and cook briefly. Then add the hot bean sauce, stir, and add chopped ginger. Stir until the meat and ginger have absorbed the red color from the hot bean sauce. Add 1 cup stock or water. Then carefully add the bean curd cubes and stir gently.

2. Allow the liquid in the *wok* to cook down somewhat, keeping it over a medium flame. Stir occasionally being careful not to break the bean curd cubes. Just before the liquid has cooked away, stir the SEASONINGS and add with the green onion. (You may add the green onion at any time from the end of To COOK: Step 1 to just before serving. It depends on whether you want the onion flavor to be cooked into the sauce or whether you want the onion flavor to be more isolated and distinct.) Stir, check for salt. The consistency should now be very thick, almost custardlike. If necessary add a Tbsp. or so more cornstarch first mixing it with a few Tbsps. of water to make a thin paste. Sprinkle ground Szechwan pepper over the bean curd. Serve hot.

NOTE: When to add the optional ingredients:

a.) If using garlic, chop a few Tbsps. very finely and add together with the ginger (To COOK: Step 1, above). If you are serving other garlic-flavored dishes, it is better to leave the garlic out of this dish.

b.) If using fermented black beans, use a very small amount and add together with the ginger (To COOK: Step 1, above).

c.) Fresh or dried mushrooms, wood ear and, especially in Japan and Hawaii, lotus-root stems find their way into this dish. Soak dried mushrooms or wood ear in warm water until softened, rinse well, cut away stems or tough portions before using. Add together with SEASONINGS (To COOK: Step 2, above).

d.) If using sesame oil, add 1 Tbsp. after mixing in the SEASONINGS (To COOK: Step 2, above).

Ma-la Dou-fu
HOT SESAME DOU-FU

麻辣豆腐

A variation of Ma-po Dou-fu.

2 cups cubed bean curd
2–3 fresh or dried red peppers
¼ lb. beef
2 tsps. finely chopped garlic
1 green onion
½ tsp. ground Szechwan pepper
1 tsp. fermented black beans
1 cup warm water
SEASONINGS
    2 tsps. cornstarch mixed with 4 tsps. water
    4 tsps. water
    2 tsps. soy sauce
    1 tsp. salt
    2 tsps. sesame oil
4–6 Tbsps. oil

TO PREPARE: 1. Carefully cut the bean curd into ¾-inch cubes. In a pot bring 4 cups water to boil. Add the bean curd to the boiling water and continue boiling until the cubes float to the surface. (This makes the bean curd less likely to crumble.)

2. Seed the red peppers and chop them finely. If using dried red peppers, soak them in warm water until softened, then seed and chop them finely. Chop the beef and garlic finely. Cut the green onion into small sections or chop it finely.

3. In a cup or small bowl, mix the SEASONINGS, first dissolving the cornstarch in the water and then mixing in the other ingredients.

TO COOK: 1. Heat 4–6 Tbsps. cooking oil in a *wok* or large frying pan until very hot. Add the chopped beef and stir-fry for 30 seconds or so. Add the red pepper, garlic and ground Szechwan pepper and stir-fry briefly. Then add the warm water, bean curd cubes and fermented black beans. Stir gently. Bring to a boil then reduce the heat.

2. Stir the SEASONINGS and add to the *wok*. Stir and check for salt. Remove to a serving bowl and serve hot.

Jia-chang Dou-fu
HOME–STYLE DEEP–FRIED DOU-FU

家常豆腐

As one might expect, there are any number of ways to prepare Home-style Deep-fried Dou-fu. The following recipe is typical of western China. This dish is slightly hot but you can make it hotter by increasing the hot bean sauce or by adding a few seeded and sliced fresh red peppers. If you want a milder dish, reduce the measure of hot bean sauce or omit it entirely.

3–4 cups cubed bean curd, about 1½ Japanese-style bean curd cakes or 3–4 smaller Chinese-style cakes
¼–½ lb. pork
1 tsp. dry cornstarch
1–2 Tbsps. hot bean sauce, according to taste
1–2 green onions
1 tsp. finely chopped ginger
1 Tbsp. coarsely chopped garlic
1 tsp. fermented black beans
SEASONINGS
    1 Tbsp. rice wine or dry sherry
    2 Tbsps. soy sauce
    1 tsp. salt
    ½ tsp. sugar
    1 cup pork or chicken stock or water
1 Tbsps. cornstarch mixed with 2 Tbsps. water
approximately 1¼ cups oil

TO PREPARE: 1. Cut the bean curd into 1-inch cubes. Heat 1 cup of cooking oil in a *wok* or large frying pan until very hot. Add the bean curd cubes, a few pieces at a time, slowly deep frying them over a medium–high flame until all sides turn a golden color. Remove and drain. Empty the excess oil from the *wok*. Some will be used for TO COOK: Step 1, below, but for directions on how to reclaim cooking oil, see page 30.

2. Cut the pork into bite-sized pieces. I prefer thin slices, about as long and as wide as the bean curd cubes. Dust the pork pieces with the cornstarch and set aside.

3. Cut the green onion into 1-inch lengths or chop it fine. Chop the ginger fine and the garlic coarsely.

4. Mix the SEASONINGS in a small bowl.

TO COOK: 1. Heat 6 Tbsps. of the cooking oil in a *wok* or large frying pan until very hot. Add the pork and cook until the pork has turned white. Then add the ginger, garlic and hot bean sauce. When the aroma of the garlic and hot bean sauce becomes pronounced (a matter of a few seconds), add the SEASONINGS. Stir.

2. Carefully add the pieces of deep-fried bean curd, the green onion and fermented black beans. Stir gently. Reduce the flame to low and simmer until the liquid has cooked down somewhat. Then stir the cornstarch which has been mixed with water and add to the *wok*. Check for salt. Remove **to a serving bowl** and serve hot.

Fan-qie Huang-gua
ZUCCHINI AND TOMATOES

蕃茄黄瓜

Huang-gua (黄瓜) is a type of squash similar to cucumber and is common in China. It is this vegetable that is actually called for in this and the other squash recipes. However, Western-type zucchini is very similar to huang-gua and in these recipes zucchini tastes just as good. Not at all hot, this dish is best if the zucchini and tomatoes are garden fresh.

1–1½ lbs. zucchini
4–5 average-sized tomatoes or
   3 large ones
1½ tsps. salt
1½ cups chicken or pork stock
1 Tbsp. cornstarch mixed with
   2 Tbsps. water
approximately ½ cup oil

TO PREPARE: 1. Wash and clean the zucchini and cut off the ends. If desired, peel off the skin. Cut the zucchini lengthwise into quarters and cut each into 1½-inch lengths.
2. Wash and stem the tomatoes. Blanch the tomatoes in boiling water for 2 or 3 minutes, then remove and gently peel the skin from the tomatoes. Cut each tomato into eighths.

TO COOK: 1. Heat 4–6 Tbsps. of the cooking oil in a *wok* or large frying pan until very hot. Add the zucchini and ½ tsp. salt. Stir-fry until the zucchini is slightly softened. Remove and drain.
2. Heat 2 Tbsps. of the cooking oil in the *wok* until very hot. Add the tomato sections and stir-fry carefully for 20–30 seconds. Remove and drain.
3. Add the stock to the *wok* and bring to a boil. Reduce the heat to low. Add the remaining 1 tsp. salt. Stir. Then add the cornstarch mixed with the water to thicken the stock.
4. To serve, place the zucchini pieces in the center of a bowl and arrange the tomatoes attractively around them. Pour the hot, thickened seasoned stock over the vegetables and serve hot.

Cu Liu Huang-gua
HOT AND SOUR ZUCCHINI

醋溜黃瓜

In cooked dishes like this one, zucchini is a substitute for the Chinese vegetable huang-gua *that is generally unavailable in the West. This is one of the few recipes that uses sesame oil for cooking rather than for flavoring. Very spicy, sour and hot, yet very fresh tasting.*

½ lb. zucchini
2 tsps. finely chopped fresh ginger
2 tsps. finely chopped green onion
2 dried red peppers
1 tsp. Szechwan peppercorns
SEASONINGS
    1 tsp. cornstarch
    1 Tbsp. Chinese red vinegar or Chinese white vinegar
    1 tsp. soy sauce
    2 tsps. sugar
4 Tbsps. sesame oil

TO PREPARE: 1. Wash the zucchini and slice it into thin rounds, about ¼-inch thick. If the center is pithy, discard. Sprinkle with salt and allow to stand at least 10 minutes. Then wash and pat dry.
2. Chop the ginger and green onion very finely. Cut the stems off the dried red peppers and shake out the seeds. Slice the red peppers lengthwise into thin strips.
3. In a cup or small bowl, mix the SEASONINGS, first mixing the cornstarch with the vinegar and soy sauce and then adding the sugar.

TO COOK: 1. Heat 4 Tbsps. sesame oil in a *wok* or large frying pan until hot. Be careful not to let it burn. Add the Szechwan peppercorns and then the dried red peppers and stir-fry briefly.
2. Add the zucchini, ginger and green onion. Toss for a 20–30 seconds, then stir and add the SEASONINGS. Mix well.
3. Continue to stir-fry for a few more seconds. Make sure the zucchini is tender. Check for salt. Remove to a serving dish and serve hot.

San-se Su-cai
THREE-COLOR VEGETABLES

三色素菜

The three colors from which this dish takes its name are green from the cabbage or celery, white from the bamboo shoot and red from the tomatoes, so if you add carrots and the color orange to this dish, strictly speaking, its name becomes si-se su-cai, or "four-color vegetables." Because this dish and its variations are so universal to Chinese cooking, it probably can't be equated with any single regional cuisine. No spices are used in the preparation, so the flavor depends entirely upon the freshness of the vegetables and the richness of the stock. If cai-xin (菜心), *a type of vegetable, is available at a Chinese grocery store, use that. Otherwise use Chinese cabbage or celery.*

1 lb. *cai-xin* or Chinese cabbage or celery
3 small tomatoes, or 2 large ones

TO PREPARE: 1. If you have *cai-xin*, clean and cut off its root portion and place the vegetable in boiling water for about 1 minute. Remove and cool by rinsing under cold water. Drain

1 cup bamboo shoot
1 carrot (optional)
4–5 dried or fresh mushrooms
1 cup stock (pork, chicken or a
    mixture of both)
1 tsp. salt
1 tsp. sugar
$1\frac{1}{2}$ tsps. cornstarch mixed with
    3 tsps. water
3 Tbsps. rendered chicken fat
2–3 Tbsps. oil

and cut into bite-sized pieces. Or wash and clean the Chinese cabbage or celery. Cut into $1\frac{1}{2}$-inch sections, discarding the celery tops if that is the green vegetable you are using.

2. Blanch the tomatoes in boiling water for 2–3 minutes, then remove their skins and cut into quarters or smaller sections. Remove as many seeds as possible.

3. If you are using sliced canned bamboo shoot, wash and drain it. If the slices are very large, you might cut them into bite-sized pieces. If using fresh bamboo shoot, cut it into $\frac{1}{4}$-inch slices and then into pieces about 1-inch by 2-inches. Peel the carrot and cut into pieces slightly thinner than the bamboo shoot slices.

4. Soak the dried mushrooms in warm water until softened, cut away the tough stems and then use them whole or cut them in half. If using fresh mushrooms, rinse and stem them.

To cook: 1. Heat 3 Tbsps. of cooking oil in a *wok* or large frying pan over high or medium high heat. If using carrots, begin by adding them to the oil and stir-frying them briefly. Add the *cai-xin* or Chinese cabbage or celery, then immediately add the stock salt, and sugar. Cook until you can smell the greens, then remove and drain and arrange on a serving plate. Leave the stock in the *wok*.

2. Over a medium heat, add the mushrooms to the stock in the *wok*. Cook until you can smell the mushrooms, then remove and drain and arrange with the greens on the serving plate. Next, add the bamboo shoots to the stock and cook gently until you can smell the bamboo. Remove, drain, arrange with the other ingredients on the serving dish. Finally, add the tomatoes to the stock and cook gently for only a very brief time. Remove, drain and arrange on the serving dish.*

3. When all the ingredients have been cooked, stir and add the cornstarch and water mixture to the stock that remains in the *wok*. Stir. Add the rendered chicken fat and heat briefly. Stir. Then pour this sauce over the vegetables on the serving dish and serve hot.

* If you want to try something more formal, keep the vegetables separate on the serving plate, arranging them to show their contrasting colors.

SOUPS

Soups are an integral part of almost every Chinese meal. However, most soups are served at the end —not at the beginning—and their function seems to be to help settle the foods which have been eaten during the other courses. In this sense, Chinese soups may be thought of more as a meat-flavored tea served after meals than as a soup in the Western sense. Almost all are light, rather thin broths, saltier than Western soups, to which may be added shreds of meat or poultry, greens, *dou-fu*, vegetables, or Chinese noodles. (See page 116, for suggestions on how to make Chinese soup with leftovers). There are, of course, heavier and more elaborate Chinese soups that are usually served as a regular course in addition to and prior to the light soup which ends the meal.

Huo-tui Dong-gua Tang
HAM AND WINTER–MELON SOUP 火腿冬瓜湯

If you can find imported Yunnan canned ham, use it, but domestic canned ham is just as good. Whole fresh winter melon looks like a large muskmelon (though the taste is very different) and is frequently sold already sectioned in Oriental grocery stores.

$\frac{1}{8}$ lb. ham
$\frac{1}{3}$ lb. section of winter melon
4 cups chicken stock
1 tsp. salt
$\frac{1}{4}$ tsp. black pepper (optional)

To PREPARE: Cut the ham into thin slices and then into strips about $\frac{1}{4}$-inch wide. Peel the skin off the winter melon and remove the pith or other fibrous material from its interior. Cut the winter melon into thin strips, about 1 to 2-inches long, 1-inch wide and $\frac{1}{8}$-inch thick.

To COOK: In a *wok* or pot, heat the stock. (For a basic stock recipe, see page 115.) Add ham, winter melon and salt. Simmer for 15–20 minutes, or until the melon strips become translucent and tender. Check for salt, add pepper if desired, and remove to a tureen. Serve hot.

NOTE: As it cooks, the winter melon will thicken the soup slightly, so there is no need to add another thickening agent.

KOREAN HOT BEEF AND VEGETABLE SOUP

This recipe is a variation of a Korean soup based on beef, green onion and a red-pepper sauce that is very similar to Szechwan's hot bean sauce.

¼–½ lb. stewing beef
3 green onions
3 dried mushrooms
1 tsp. finely chopped garlic
4–6 Tbsps. cooking oil
1–2 tsps. hot bean sauce
6–8 cups stock (chicken, pork, or pork and chicken) or water
1–2 Tbsps. soy sauce
2 tsps. salt
2 tsps. rice wine or dry sherry
½ tsp. black pepper
1 tsp. sesame oil

To PREPARE: 1. Cut the beef into bite-sized pieces.
2. Cut the green onions into 3-inch lengths and then slice each in half lengthwise so that the layers of the green onion will separate while cooking.
3. Soak the dried mushrooms in warm water until softened, cut away the tough stems and then into shreds. Chop the garlic fine.

To COOK: 1. Heat 4–6 Tbsps. cooking oil in a *wok* or large heavy pot until very hot. Add the beef pieces and stir-fry until the meat is lightly browned.
2. Add the garlic and green onion and hot bean sauce and stir-fry for a few moments. Then add the mushrooms, stock or water, soy sauce, salt, wine and black pepper. Stir. (For a basic stock recipe, see page 115.)
3. Bring to a boil, then reduce the heat and simmer for 10–15 minutes. Check for salt, stir in the sesame oil, remove to a tureen and serve hot.

Zha-cai Rou-si Tang

搾菜肉絲湯

SZECHWAN-VEGETABLE AND PORK-SHRED SOUP
COLOR: page 38

This strong-tasting soup is very easy to make. The Szechwan vegetable makes the soup hot and rather salty so never add salt or use presalted stock.

¼–½ lb. pork, thinly sliced
¼–½ lb. Szechwan vegetable*
4 cups stock (chicken, pork, or pork and chicken)

*Keep in mind that the more Szechwan vegetable you use, the saltier and hotter the soup will be.

To PREPARE: 1. Shred the pork. To facilitate cutting, you may want to parboil the meat first.
2. Wash the reddish pickling material off the Szechwan vegetable. Cut it into thin slices and then into shreds.

To COOK: 1. In a *wok* or pot, heat the stock to boiling. (For a basic stock recipe, see page 115.) Reduce to a simmer and add pork and Szechwan vegetable. Cook for 5–10 minutes. Check for salt. It may be necessary to dilute the soup by adding boiling water. Remove to a tureen and serve.

Suan-la Tang
HOT AND SOUR SOUP
COLOR: page 34

酸辣湯

Hot and Sour Soup is one of the best known of all Szechwanese recipes in the West. Basic Suan-la Tang *is simply a light stock flavored with vinegar and pepper and thickened with cornstarch. Pork and chicken shreds, bean curd, dried mushrooms, wood ear, dried chicken or duck's blood, sea cucumber and fish stomach are all common additions. However, some of these exotic ingredients are difficult to obtain outside China. The following recipe uses familiar ingredients and others that are generally available at Chinese provisions stores.*

¼ lb. shredded chicken and/or pork

3–4 dried mushrooms

3–4 pieces wood ear (optional)

1 cake bean curd

¼ cup bamboo shoot (optional)

2 Tbsps. finely chopped green onion

1 tsp. finely chopped fresh ginger (optional)

4½ tsps.–2 Tbsps. cornstarch mixed with 3–4 Tbsps. water

1½ Tbsps. vinegar

1½ Tbsps. water

½ tsp. black or white pepper

1 egg

1 tsp. salt

1 Tbsp. ketchup

1 Tbsp. soy sauce

1 tbsp. sesame oil (optional)

6 cups chicken or pork stock

TO PREPARE: 1. Shred the chicken and/or pork. To facilitate cutting, you may want to parboil the meat first.

2. Soak the dried mushrooms and wood ear in warm water until softened, rinse thoroughly and cut off the tough stems of the mushrooms and any tough section of wood ear. Shred mushrooms and wood ear.

3. Carefully cut the *dou-fu*, or bean curd, into thin strips or shreds. Shred the bamboo shoot. Chop the green onion and ginger finely.

4. Mix the cornstarch with the water in a cup. Mix the vinegar and water and pepper in another cup. Beat the egg lightly in a bowl. Set these aside.

TO COOK: 1. Heat the stock in a *wok* or pot. (For a basic stock recipe, see page 115.) Add all shredded and chopped ingredients except the green onion. (TO PREPARE: Steps 1 and 2, above.)

2. Bring to a boil and add the salt, ketchup and soy sauce. Giving the cornstarch mixed with water a stir, add that. Stir and return to a boil.

3. Reduce the flame somewhat and stir in the lightly beaten egg. When the egg has coalesced into many fine threads, remove the soup to a tureen.

4. Now add the vinegar-water-pepper mixture, a little at a time to taste, stirring between additions. You should use most, if not all, of the prepared mixture, but the final effect of hotness and sourness is up to you. Finally add the green onion and sesame oil. Stir briefly and serve hot.

Ji-pian Tang
CHICKEN-SLICE SOUP

½ lb. chicken breast
MARINADE
    2 tsps. cornstarch mixed
    with 4 tsps. water
    1 egg white
3–4 dried mushroom
⅛ lb. ham (optional)
4 cups stock (chicken, pork, or
    pork and chicken)
1 tsp. salt
¼ tsp. black pepper (optional)

TO PREPARE: 1. Cut the chicken breast into thin slices, about 1-inch wide and 2-inches long. Make the MARINADE by mixing the cornstarch with the water and then beating in the egg white. Mix with the chicken slices and let stand 10 minutes. 2. Soak the dried mushrooms in warm water until softened, cut away tough stems and cut into thin slices. Cut the ham into thin slices and then into strips about ¼-inch wide.

TO COOK: 1. Boil 2–4 cups water in a *wok* or pot and add the chicken slices a few at a time and cook very briefly. When the chicken turns white remove to a tureen. Discard the water. 2. In a *wok* or pot, heat the stock. (For a basic stock recipe, see page 115.) Add the mushroom and ham, salt and pepper. Bring to a boil and simmer for a few minutes, then pour over the chicken slices in the tureen. Check for salt and serve hot.

NOODLES

Noodles are probably the simplest way by which wheat flour can be made into something you can eat. You can, of course, make them yourself, but where you can buy fresh noodles I would strongly advise buying them. And where you can't, I suggest buying dried noodles (which are fine for soups, if not for fried noodles).

Noodle dough has to be kneaded well to be good, and it is denser than most bread doughs. The Chinese have developed various mechanical arrangements to facilitate kneading such dense dough, none of which are particularly easy to simulate in a Western kitchen. If you really want to make noodles, however, have are two basic recipes, which are to be used in soups rather than for fried noodles.

EGG NOODLES: Beat two eggs together and mix with 2 cups sifted all-purpose flour, adding a little water if necessary. Knead until the mixture reaches an even and pliable doughlike consistency, then cover with a damp cloth and put aside in a draft-free place to sit for a half an hour or so. Knead again, then roll out on a floured board. Thickness may vary according to personal preference but $\frac{1}{8}$ inch is about right for most uses. Carefully roll up the sheet or fold it and cut through to make the noodles. Refrigerate or keep in a cool place if you do not use them right away. If desired, add $\frac{1}{2}$ tsp. salt to the sifted flour.

BASIC (NON-EGG) NOODLES: Same Egg Noodle recipe as above but omit eggs and use water.

Man-tou
STEAMED BREAD
COLOR: page 34

饅 頭

Steamed bread, or Man-tou, and other baked goods such as meat-filled or sweet-bean-filled buns, cookies and nut bars can usually be purchased at a Chinese bakery, sometimes at a Chinese grocery store or even at Chinese restaurants. Simply reheat the bread or buns in a rice-cooker or steamer before serving.

3 cups sifted all-purpose flour
1 cup warm water
3 tsps. dry yeast

TO PREPARE: 1. In a large bowl, sprinkle the yeast and sugar the warm water. Mix after 2–3 minutes and allow to stand for 10–15 minutes, or until the yeast mixture begins to bubble.

2 tsps. sugar
1 tsp. salt
1 tsp. baking powder

2. Add sifted flour and salt and mix to form a dough. Knead until the dough is smooth and of even consistency, then cover with a damp cloth and put aside, away from any draft, to rise for 2–3 hours, or until it has doubled in bulk.

3. Punch the bread down to its original size and add the baking powder. Knead thoroughly. Cover once again and let stand for 20–30 minutes. Knead again briefly and divide the dough into small handful-sized portions. Form each into a smooth-topped ovoid bun about 2-inches in diameter and place in a steamer.

To COOK: Steam the bread for about 20 minutes. Serve hot. (For directions on how to improvise a steamer, see page 22.)

Hong-shao Niu-rou Mian
BRAISED BEEF NOODLES

紅燒牛肉麵

In China, you would be just as likely to eat this as a snack at a small street stall or vending cart as to order it in a restaurant or to make it at home. Buy freshly made, wide, thick noodles at a Chinese grocery store or substitute your own homemade egg noodles (see page 106). This recipe makes 5 to 6 individual bowls.

Braised Beef (see page 62)
1 lb. fresh noodles

To PREPARE: 1. Make the Braised Beef, or *Hong-shau Niu-rou*, as directed on page 62, except in To COOK: Step 2, use 4–6 cups more water or stock and allow the stew to simmer 1 hour longer (To COOK: Step 3).

2. In a large *wok* or pot, bring at least 1 gallon water to boil. Divide the fresh noodles into 5 or 6 portions and separate any strands that have stuck together. Place in the boiling water. Cooking time will depend on the thickness of the noodles. They should be tender but not mushy.

To SERVE: 1. When the noodles are done, remove each portion with a wire strainer and chopsticks and place each in a bowl. (If enough water is used to cook the noodles, it is not necessary to rinse the noodles. If a gallon or less water was used, it may be advisable to rinse the noodles briefly in tepid water). Add a few pieces of beef to each bowl of noodles and fill the bowl with beef broth. Szechwan-style hot pepper sauce, or *la-jiao jiang*, may be served on the side.

Ma-yi Shang Shu

蝦蟻上樹

"ANTS CLIMBING A TREE"
TRANSPARENT VERMICELLI WITH PORK AND HOT BEAN SAUCE
COLOR: page 36

This dish gets its name because the fen-tiao, *or transparent vermicelli, which is stained a reddish brown with the hot bean sauce, soy sauce and meat juices, is said to resemble tree bark while the tiny pieces of finely chopped pork supposedly look like ants. Of course, you are free to visualize it any way you like, and perhaps a more appetizing way is to think of this dish as being similar to* Ma-po Dou-fu *with the vermicelli replacing the* dou-fu. *Since the transparent vermicelli is purchased dried, it can be bought in quantity and stored indefinitely. An immensely popular dish, there are many versions of this basic recipe. This dish is very hot.*

¼ lb. transparent vermicelli (sold in skeins of varying weight. Examine the label and estimate the correct amount.)
¼ lb. pork
2–3 Tbsps. finely chopped green onion
1 Tbsp. finely chopped fresh ginger
1–2 Tbsps. hot bean sauce
SEASONINGS
    1 Tbsp. rice wine or dry sherry
    1 Tbsp. soy sauce
    1–2 tsps. salt, depending on the saltiness of the hot bean sauce
    1 cup stock or water
4–6 Tbsps. cooking oil
OPTIONAL
    2–3 fresh or dried red peppers
    2–3 dried mushrooms
    ½ green pepper

TO PREPARE: 1. Soften the vermicelli by soaking it in warm water briefly. When the threads become transparent and soft, remove and drain. Place the vermicelli on a chopping board and cut through it several times with the cleaver. If the vermicelli is not cut, it is almost impossible to separate later or to eat with any degree of finesse.
2. Chop the pork, green onion and ginger finely.
3. In a bowl, mix the SEASONINGS.

TO COOK: 1. Heat 4–6 Tbsps. cooking oil in a *wok* or large frying pan until hot. Add the pork pieces and toss over high heat until the pork is gray.
2. Immediately add the green onion, ginger and hot bean sauce. Stir well. When the pork and ginger have absorbed the red color from the hot bean sauce and the aroma of the hot bean sauce is strong, add the SEASONINGS.
3. Reduce the flame, stir once, and add the vermicelli. Simmer, stirring occasionally, until the liquid has cooked down. Check for salt, remove to a serving bowl, and serve hot.

NOTE: When to add the optional ingredients.
a.) Top and seed the red peppers and chop them finely. If using dried red peppers, soak in warm water until softened, then seed and chop them. Add together with the green onion, ginger and hot bean sauce (TO COOK: Step 2, above).
b.) Soak the dried mushrooms in warm water until softened, cut away the tough stems, and cut the mushrooms into ½-inch pieces. Add together with the SEASONINGS (TO COOK: Step 3, above).
c.) Top and seed the green pepper and cut the pepper into shreds. Fry momentarily in 1 Tbsp. very hot cooking oil in another *wok* or frying pan with a pinch of salt. Add just before serving (TO COOK: Step 3, above).

Dan Dan Mian

坦坦麺

"DAN-DAN" NOODLES
NOODLES WITH PEANUTS, SESAME PASTE AND HOT SAUCE

Like Braised Beef Noodles, this is an inexpensive snack dish, which you would normally eat at a stand or stall. Ideally the beef broth from Braised Beef would be used (see page 62). For the purpose of making this dish, however, a mock Braised Beef broth may be made according to the directions below. Buy fresh noodles at the Chinese grocery store or make your own (see page 106). With the exception of the ingredients for the mock broth, all measures of ingredients are per serving.

1 cup Braised Beef broth per serving, or 1 cup MOCK BROTH per serving

MOCK BROTH (for 4 servings)

1 cup beef bouillon
1 piece star anise
4–6 Szechwan peppercorns
½–1 green onion, cut into 2-inch sections
1 Tbsp. hot bean sauce
1 slice ginger
1 Tbsp. rice wine or dry sherry
1 clove garlic, crushed

¼ lb. fresh noodles, per serving
1–2 Tbsps. finely chopped garlic
2 tsps.–1 Tbsp. finely chopped fresh ginger
1 Tbsp. soy sauce
1 Tbsp. finely chopped green onion
1 tsp. salt
2–3 Tbsps. oil, lard or rendered suet
2 Tbsps. sesame paste
1–2 Tbsps. hot pepper sauce, or 1–2 Tbsps. red oil (reduce the measure of oil or lard proportionately)
1 tsp. crushed peanuts

TO PREPARE: 1. Make the broth by adding the MOCK BROTH ingredients to the beef bouillon and simmer for 30 minutes. Remove the star anise, ginger and green onion sections before combining the broth with the noodles.

2. Chop the green onion, ginger and garlic finely. Crush or grind the peanuts to a powder.

3. In a large *wok* or pot, bring at least 1 gallon of water to boil. Divide the noodles into equal portions and separate any strands that have stuck together. Place in the boiling water. Cooking time will depend on the thickness of the noodles. They should be tender but not mushy.

TO SERVE: 1. While the noodles are cooking, put the remaining ingredients, except the crushed peanuts, into individual, medium-sized bowls. Mix.

2. When the noodles are cooked, remove each portion with a wire strainer and chopsticks and place each in a bowl on top of the other ingredients. Top with the powdered peanuts. Serve hot. Each person should mix the contents of his bowl. The resulting dish should be like spaghetti with a thick and sticky sauce.

SWEETS

In China it is the soup rather than a dessert or sweet that finishes off the meal. Desserts and sweets, if they are to be eaten at all, tend to be associated with festivals, banquet cooking or in-between-meal treats, and they are not necessarily provided at the end of every meal. At a normal meal, if a "sweet" is served after the soup course, it is likely to be fresh fruit, which takes no time to prepare and is a healthy, natural food.

Xin-ren Dou-fu
ALMOND GELATIN

杏仁豆腐

5 tsps. powdered, unflavored gelatin
2 cups water
1 cup milk
1 Tbsp. almond extract
SYRUP
    2 cups water
    1 cup sugar
    ½ cup milk
Sectioned fresh canned fruit (optional—as desired)

TO PREPARE: 1. Soften the gelatin in ¼–½ cup of the water. Bring the remaining water to a boil and add the gelatin-water mixture and stir until the gelatin is thoroughly dissolved. Add the milk and the almond extract and stir well. Pour the mixture into a large bowl or pan and refrigerate until set (several hours).

2. Mix the SYRUP in a medium-sized container and chill.

TO ASSEMBLE: Remove the set gelatin from the bowl and cut it into small, ¾-inch cubes. Pour the syrup over the cubes in a large serving bowl. If desired, stir in bite-sized fresh or canned fruits. Serve in the large bowl and provide individual bowls and Chinese soup spoons.

NOTE: A heated version of this dish may be made using *dou-fu,* or bean curd. Cut the bean curd into ¾-inch cubes and boil in water until the cubes float to the surface. Remove and drain. To make the SYRUP, use the same ingredients at left but heat the water and the sugar in a saucepan and stir until just before it begins to boil. Remove from the heat and allow to cool slightly. Then add 1 Tbsp. almond extract and the milk. Stir well. Pour the syrup over the heated *dou-fu* cubes in a large serving bowl and serve hot.

Ba-si Ping-guo
DEEP–FRIED CANDIED APPLES

拔絲蘋果

This is a standard Chinese dessert recipe. The batter-coated apples are deep fried, covered with hot syrup and then dipped in ice water to harden the candy coating. Getting the consistency and temperature of the syrup right is sometimes difficult without a candy thermometer, and cleaning the hardened sugar mixture from pans and utensils is somewhat of a chore. If this dish is made with bananas instead of apples, it is called Ba-si Xiang-jiao (拔絲香蕉).

1 lb. eating apples, or bananas
BATTER
    ¾ cup flour
    ¼ cup cornstarch
    ½ cup water
    2–3 egg whites
SYRUP
    1½ cups sugar
    ¾ cup water
    ¼ cup sesame oil
    2 tsps. black sesame seeds
4 cups ice water
oil for deep frying

TO PREPARE: 1. To make the BATTER, first mix the flour and cornstarch with the water and then beat in the egg whites. The BATTER should be very thick.

2. Peel and core the apples and cut them into eighths. If using bananas, peel and cut diagonally into pieces comparable in size to apple eighths.

3. Mix the SYRUP in a medium-sized saucepan.

TO COOK: 1. On one burner, start to heat about 3–4 cups cooking oil in a *wok* or deep fryer. At the same time, on another burner, heat the SYRUP in the saucepan, stirring the mixture only until the sugar is completely dissolved. When the SYRUP starts to darken slightly, reduce the heat. Check the consistency by dropping a small amount into a cup of ice water. If it forms a hard ball which does not flatten when removed from the water, the SYRUP is ready. If using black sesame seeds, mix in with the syrup before proceeding to the next step.

2. Add 5–8 apple or banana pieces to the BATTER and coat thoroughly. Deep fry until the pieces turn a medium-golden brown. Remove the pieces from the oil, drain, and stir them into the SYRUP. Then, one by one, drop the pieces into the ice water. Keep the pieces separate. Remove almost immediately, and arrange on a serving platter. Proceed to prepare the remaining apple or banana pieces in this manner and when all have been deep fried and candied, serve. (For directions on how to reclaim the cooking oil, see page 30.)

Ba-si Zhi-you Zhi-ma

拔絲脂油芝麻

DEEP–FRIED CANDIED BACON WITH SESAME

This recipe originally called for zhi-you, a kind of pork fat. Substitute unsmoked bacon or try using smoked bacon.

½ lb. unsmoked sliced bacon
BATTER
    ½ cup flour
    ½ cup cornstarch
    ½ cup water
    2 egg whites
    ½ tsp. salt
SYRUP
    1 cup sugar
    ½ cup water
    ¼ cup sesame oil
4 cups ice water
oil for deep frying

TO PREPARE: 1. Cut bacon strips into quarters and either roll each loosely or use as a piece.

2. To make the BATTER, first mix the flour and cornstarch with the water and then beat in the egg whites. Finally add the salt. The BATTER should be very thick.

3. Mix the SYRUP in a medium-sized saucepan.

TO COOK: 1. Heat 2 cups or so cooking oil in a *wok* or deep fryer over a medium flame. When the oil is heated, dip the bacon rolls into the BATTER and then deep fry, a few at a time, until the bacon rolls turn a deep golden brown. Keep the flame low so that the pieces deep fry slowly and the bacon is cooked thoroughly. As each batch finishes, remove and drain. (For directions on how to reclaim cooking oil, see page 30.)

2. Heat the SYRUP in the saucepan, stirring only until the sugar is dissolved. When the SYRUP starts to darken slightly, reduce the heat. Check the consistency by dropping a small amount into a cup of ice water. If it forms a hard ball which does not flatten when removed from the water, the SYRUP is ready.

3. Add the deep-fried bacon rolls to the SYRUP and stir together. Then, to harden the coating, one by one drop the sugared bacon pieces into the ice water. Keep the pieces separate. Remove immediately, arrange on a serving platter and serve.

SURVIVAL COOKING

If economy is a crucial factor—or a factor at all—in the foods you choose to eat, you can use some of these money-saving techniques in your kitchen. The following pages elaborate these principles with basic recipes for rice and leftovers, but the notes below outline some economy measures which I have found convenient.

1. Simply reduce the amount of food prepared per person and eat more rice. Time-tested. When there is plenty to go around, the recipes in this book are designed to feed 1–2 persons and, with a moderate consumption of rice, there may be some leftovers.
2. In dishes where meat in a major ingredient, simply reduce the amount of meat. In China, *dou-fu*, or bean curd, is often used as a meat substitute, but it is not as readily available in the U.S. and may cost as much per gram of protein as meat.
3. Use cheap salad oil instead of peanut oil for cooking.
4. Make up dishes using local vegetables or whatever is in season.
5. In chicken dishes, substitute wings or backs for the more expensive breast meat. It tastes just as good, some say better, and the time it takes to chew the meat off the bone slows down the meal and makes it seem like more. Just hack the bone, skin, everything, into bite-sized pieces and proceed as usual but allow slightly more cooking time.
6. Combine compatible leftovers and create new versions of fried rice, maybe adding some scrambled egg and green onion (chopped and briefly stir-fried before adding to the main ingredients).
7. Make soup or stock out of leftovers, especially bones.

BASIC RICE

You may find that you can buy better and less expensive rice in bulk at an Oriental grocery store than at the supermarket. Long-grain rice, which is a bit firmer and which requires more water for cooking, is usually more available than oval or short-grain rice, which needs less water to cook and is more moist. Whichever kind of rice you use, the results of your efforts should neither be too dry nor too mushy. Rice should never be lumpy or sticky. The serving should look "fluffy" and the grains of rice should be separate from each other. Since rice expands as it cooks or steams, about $\frac{1}{2}$ cup of raw rice per serving is usually about right.

Remove all excess starch by thoroughly washing the rice before cooking or steaming. Under cold running water, rinse the rice either in a large bowl or in a colander set in a pan or bowl. With your hands or with a spoon, stir the rice grains around. Continue this until the cold water running off the rice is fairly clear, not milky. Do not let the rice stand in water to "wash" because it only absorbs water, the starches remain, and the taste is bad. Wash the rice just before you are going to cook it.

Of course, a rice cooker makes perfect rice every time—just follow the directions that come with this appliance and make adjustments in amounts of water to add depending on the type of rice you are using and your personal preference. If you are using a regular pot, follow this method: Place the washed rice evenly in the bottom of the pot. Add cold water. (*1 cup raw long-grain rice needs about 1-½ cups water; 1 cup oval-grain rice needs 1 cup water.* Follow these basic proportions but adjust to personal preference.) Cover the pot. Over a medium-high heat bring to a boil and boil for 5 minutes, maybe turning the heat down to medium in the last minute or so. Most of the liquid should be absorbed. Quickly but gently give the rice a stir to keep it from sticking to the bottom and to insure even cooking. Turn the flame to very low and cook, covered —don't lift the lid or do any stirring or a lot of necessary steam will be lost—for 20 minutes or so. Turn off the heat. Let stand for 15 minutes. Before serving, fluff and separate the rice grains with a fork or chopsticks. Serve hot. Rice is usually eaten as is, not dotted with butter or drenched in soy sauce which turns the rice an unappetizing color.

For steamed rice, the method is to place the washed rice in a pan with quite a bit of water. Boil vigorously for 5 minutes and drain and discard water. Spread the rice in a thin layer on cheesecloth and place in a bamboo steamer. Make sure there are a few small holes for the steam to pass through—pierce the cheesecloth with a fork. Cover and steam over a medium flame for 20 minutes or so. An alternate method is to place the washed and boiled rice in individual heat-proof serving bowls, adding the water to each bowl (according the proportions in italics above). Steam, covered, on a rack for 1½ hours.

FRIED RICE

Fried rice, as far as I'm concerned, should be thought of as a way to use leftovers or to make a quick lunch out of odds and ends. Thus, a recipe as such seems out of place. The basic principle is to use cold cooked rice—I save the leftover rice from each evening's meal in a plastic container in the refrigerator. The rice should be heated in the *wok* or a frying pan with a bit of oil first. While the rice is being warmed up, prepare the other things you will use. If you have a large amount of any one dish left over, base the fried rice dish on that and add additional fresh ingredients—ginger, meat, green onion—which will supplement or complement the leftover. You can always add carrot (diced and stir-fried), celery (diced and stir-fried) and egg or egg yolk (lightly beaten, fried and stirred during frying to break it up).

For example, if you have leftovers from a pork dish, 1) start heating the rice, 2) if necessary cut up a small amount of additional pork, 3) finely chop some ginger, 4) chop up some green onions, 5) chop up any other vegetables you have that you think can be used. When the rice is well heated, remove to a serving bowl. Cook the egg first, and place it with the rice. Then stir-fry carrots or other firm vegetables, and place these with the rice. Finally fry any fresh meat, adding some chopped ginger. Then add the leftovers, warming them up thoroughly, and return the rice and egg to the *wok*, stir well, and add chopped green onion. Add about 1 tsp. salt for every large serving of cooked rice. Season and color by adding soy sauce, a small amount of wine, black pepper, a small amount of sugar and vinegar. If desired, sprinkle sesame oil over the rice and stir before serving. You can make hot "Szechwan-tasting" fried rice by adding hot bean sauce to the meat, as well as red peppers or garlic.

FRIED NOODLES

Like fried rice, I think of fried noodles as a snack or a way to use leftovers. Excluding the variation found in American Chinese restaurants where a meat and vegetable and viscous cornstarch glob is poured over some sort of dry crunchy affair, there are two ways in which fried noodles are prepared. In one, the fresh noodles are boiled and then fried in a lot of oil, pressed down to the bottom of the pan so that the bottom layer becomes slightly crisp. Turn and repeat this process. The noodles are then transferred to a plate and the cooked meat and/or vegetables and sauce are poured over them. In the other method, only one pan is used. First the meat and vegetables are stir-fried, then removed from the pan. The boiled noodles are fried in the remaining flavored oil to which the cooked meat and vegetables are re-added. Add soy sauce, wine, vinegar, salt, etc., to taste. Mix well, then serve.

The size of the noodles varies considerably, from the fine vermicellilike noodles used in crispy fried noodles to the thick doughy noodles for which Shantung is famous. Fresh noodles for frying are different from fresh noodles used in soup. Inquire as to the best use when you buy fresh noodles at the Chinese grocery store.

It difficult to make fried noodles that aren't either too greasy or too mushy and that don't stick to the pan. Cooking time and amounts of oil and so forth vary depending on the size of the noodles, but in general, don't overcook the noodle while boiling it prior to frying it. When you fry it use a low fire and keep the noodles moving, unless you want to make the crispy kind of noodles, in which case a frying pan is often preferable to the *wok*.

For the meat and vegetables, literally anything will do. Most vegetables should be stir-fried separately first and put aside. Then fry the meat with ginger and replace the vegetables. If you're planning to put the meat and vegetable over crispy fried noodles, add some water or stock and seasonings (salt, soy sauce, sugar, wine vinegar, etc.) to the pan, thicken with a cornstarch and water mixture and then pour over the hot noodles. If you're at all hesitant, however, make fried rice, which almost always works and almost always tastes good.

BASIC STOCK

Many of the recipes in this book call for stock—mainly chicken or pork stock, or a mixture of pork and chicken, and sometimes fish stock. (Beef stock is never used in Chinese cooking because its flavor is too strong.) Of course, you can substitute canned or instant bouillon, or water in some cases, but the taste of the dish will be perceptibly different.

The real thing is easy to make and the ingredients are really up to you.

Stock is the liquid in which meat and bones have been slowly simmered. Stock is thicker if a whole stewing chicken or a pound of lean pork is used, and thinner if chicken, pork or fish bones are used. You may use bones left over from a *cooked* dish but the result will be a very weak stock.

The basic method is to place the meat or bones in a *wok* or large pot and cover with 8 to 12 cups of cold water. (If you are more inclined to make stock as a by-product of cooking poultry and meat, place the chicken in boiling water or lightly brown the meat before placing it in boiling water. This locks the flavor into the poultry and meat and makes it better to eat—though, of course, the stock will not be as flavorful.) Heat and when the water comes to a boil, reduce the flame and simmer. Within the first 5 minutes of simmering, fats and impurities will begin to rise to the surface and at this time you should skim them off the top. Then, cover and simmer on very low heat for 2–3 hours. Once the initial skimming of fat is done, you can turn the heat off at any time and resume the cooking later. Remove the meat and bones and add vegetables —carrots, green onion, celery, whatever. These may be large chunks or cut into smaller pieces. Simmer for 20–30 minutes, or, depending on the vegetable and the size of the piece, until the vegetables are tender. During the last 5 minutes or so of the simmering of the vegetables, add whatever seasonings you like—soy sauce, salt, maybe a table-spoon of Chinese wine—and any other ingredient you think will enrich the soup—a slice of ginger, a dried scallop, dried shrimps. Remove the vegetables and strain the liquid through cheesecloth or a fine sieve. It is important to extract the remaining fat from the liquid and this can be done in a number of ways. If you must use the stock immediately, let it cool for at least 10 minutes, then skim the fat off the top and finally gently float a small piece of absorbent paper towel over the top to catch the last bits of fat. If you aren't going to use the stock right away, let it cool and then refrigerate in a sealed container. The fat will rise to the top and will soon form a round solid at the top of the container, which is very easy to remove. Make sure the stock is cool before you seal it in a container and refrigerate it, otherwise it will sour. It will keep quite a long time, especially if you reheat it to the boiling point every 4–5 days and allow it to cool before re-refrigerating. You can also freeze stock but leave an inch or so of space at the top of every container to allow for expansion.

BASIC SOUP

The light, end-of-the-meal soups described in the introduction to the soup recipes (see page 102) are quick and simple to make. They can be made from light chicken or pork stock, a combination of these two, or fish stock. But, particularly in Chinese home-cooking, it is common to make soup from nothing more than the flavored oils remain-ing in the *wok* after meat, poultry or fish have been prepared. Add several cups of water, perhaps adding a few additional shreds of prefried meat or some greens, bring to a boil and serve hot. Alternately, you could briefly fry a few shreds of pork or chicken in the *wok*, add water and bring to a boil, season and serve. You might also add greens, vege-tables, noodles or *dou-fu*. Remember that in general the function of this type of soup is to help settle the meal, not to provide a piece de resistance.

LIST OF RECIPES

Fish and Seafood

Vegetables and Dou-fu

Soups

INDEX

cooking oil, *described*, 30
  how to reclaim, 30
cornstarch, 30
crab, with Peking sauce, 90

dessert. *See* SWEETS.
DOU-FU, *described*, 14–15
  hot with almond syrup, 110
  home-style deep-fried, 98
  Ma-po Dou-fu, 96
  with sesame oil, fermented black beans and
    chopped beef, 97
duck, stir-fried,
  with bamboo shoot and sweet bean sauce, 56
  with fresh ginger and green pepper, 56

economy. *See* survival cooking.
egg, in basic soup, 116
  noodles, 106
  with pork and wood ear, 64
eggplant, *pictured*, 33
  fried strips with yu-xiang sauce, 93
  pork-stuffed deep-fried rolls with yu-xiang
    sauce, 92
  "pureed" with sesame paste, 94

fermented black beans, *described*, 15
  in Hot Sesame Dou-fu, 97
FISH, *described*, 78
  eel, braised with bamboo shoot, 84
  fillets, deep-fried with fragrant spices, 82
  fried pieces with jiao-ma sauce, 85
  salmon, deep-fried whole with sweet and
    sour sauce, 81
  sea bass, deep-fried whole in sweet and sour
    sauce, 78
  whole, deep-fried,
    with hot sauce and spices, 80
    with sweet and sour sauce, 78
  whole, fried with green onions, 86
  whole, poached with green onion shreds, 80
  See also SEAFOOD.
five spices, *described*, 15
"four-season beans," *described*, 95
fresh ginger, *described*, 15
  how to chop, 25
  with duck and green pepper, 52

gan-bian method. See *gan-chao* method.
gan-chao method, 12
gan-shao method, 12
gao-liang. See beverages.
garlic, *how to chop*, 25
  with cold white pork, 70

gelatin. *See* almond gelatin.
ginger. *See* fresh ginger.
green onion, *pictured*, 33
  with fried whole fish, 86
  with lamb, 60
  with poached whole fish, 80
  with stir-fried pork, 70
green peppers, *pictured*, 33
  with chicken shreds and bean sprouts, 50
  with stir-fried duck and fresh ginger, 56
  with stir-fried pork, 74
guai-wei method, 12

ham, in soup with winter melon, 102
hot bean sauce, *described*, 15–16
hot pepper sauce, *described*, 16
hong-you method, 12
huang-gua, *described*, 72, 99

ingredients, identification of, 14–18, 32

jiao-ma method, 17
jointing technique for chicken, 26

kidney, pork, with snow peas and bamboo
  shoot, 76

LAMB, *described*, 59
  how to cut, 24–25
  liver with yu-xiang sauce, 59
  stir-fried with green onion, 60
liver, chicken, with straw mushrooms, 57
  lamb, with yu-xiang sauce, 60
  pork, with bamboo shoot or wood ear, 77
  pork, with yu-xiang sauce, 75

ma-la method, 12
mao-tai. See beverages.
meatballs, Szechwan-style, 66
mushrooms, dried, *described*, 16
mushrooms, straw, *described*, 16
  with chicken liver, 57

NOODLES, *described*, 14, 106
  basic recipe, 106
  egg, 106
  fried, 115
  with braised beef, 107
  with peanuts, sesame paste and hot sauce, 109
  See also transparent vermicelli.

oil, cooking. *See* cooking oil.
oil drainer, *described*, 20
orange peel, dried, *described*, 16

WEIGHTS AND MEASURES:

Quantities for recipes in this book have been noted in U.S. Standard weights and measures. For the convenience of those who do not habitually use the American system, here is some basic information about equivalents.

AVOIRDUPOIS AND METRIC WEIGHTS
(approximate)

1 ounce	=	28.4 grams
1/2 pound (8 ounces)	=	226.8 grams
1 pound (16 ounces)	=	453.6 grams
2.205 pounds	=	1 kilogram

MEASURING CUPS

1 U.S. Standard cup	=	8 fluidounces or $\frac{1}{2}$ U.S. pint (U.S. fluidounce=28.4 milliliters)
1 British Standard cup	=	10 fluidounces or $\frac{1}{2}$ Imperial pint (British fluidounce=29.6 milliliters)

MEASURING SPOONS

U.S. Standard measuring spoons are **slightly smaller** in capacity than British Standard measuring spoons.

1 U.S. Standard tablespoon	=	3 U.S. Standard teaspoons
16 U.S. Standard tablespoons	=	1 U.S. Standard cup or $\frac{1}{2}$ U.S. pint
1 British Standard tablespoon	=	3 British Standard teaspoons
16 British Standard tablespoons	=	1 British Standard cup or $\frac{1}{2}$ Imperial pint

定価1,900円 in Japan